Divine Lig

OTHER BOOKS BY PETER ROCHE DE COPPENS

Ideal Man in Classical Sociology

Spiritual Man in the Modern World

The Nature and Use of Ritual

Spiritual Perspective II: The Spiritual Dimension and Implications of Love, Sex, and Marriage

The Nature and Use of Ritual for Spiritual Attainment

The Invisible Temple

Apocalypse Now: The Challenges of our Times

The Sociological Adventure: A Holistic Perspective

Lo Sviluppo dell'Uomo Nuovo, Volume I

Lo Sviluppo dell'Uomo Nuovo, Volume II

Lo Sviluppo dell'Uomo Nuovo, Volume III

The Art of Joyful Living

Divine Light and Fire: Experiencing Esoteric Christianity

Divine Light and Love

To Nancy

Practicing Esoteric Christianity

With much light,

PETER ROCHE DE COPPENS

Peter Roche de Coppens

ELEMENT
Rockport, Massachusetts • Shaftesbury, Dorset
Brisbane, Queensland

Published in the U.S.A. In 1994 by
Element, Inc.
42 Broadway, Rockport, MA 01966

Published in Great Britain in 1994 by
Element Books Limited
Longmead, Shaftesbury, Dorset

Published in Australia in 1994 by
Element Books Ltd for
Jacaranda Wiley Ltd
33 Park Road, Milton, Brisbane, 4064

Designed by Roger Lightfoot
Cover design by Max Fairbrother

Typeset by ROM-Data Corporation Ltd., Falmouth, Cornwall.
Printed in the U.S.A. By Edwards Bros. Inc.

British Library Cataloguing-in-Publication Data available

Library of Congress Catalog Card Number available

ISBN 1-85230-475-8

This work is dedicated to Maria Teresa, whose presence, love, and support have been invaluable to me during its conception in the present form; to the United Nations and all who work within its umbrella and for its ideals; and to all my students, leaders, and friends who share the eternal Quest for the Light and who want to live Life at its very best!

Contents

Introduction

This companion volume to *Divine Light and Fire* adopts the same perspective and continues the same type of analysis proposed and utilized in that first volume: to look at one of the great world religions, Christianity (particularly in its Catholic and Orthodox traditions), from an esoteric or spiritual viewpoint, from the viewpoint of higher levels of consciousness that all human beings can awaken and work with. The major aim of both volumes is to provide a creative bridge, or living connection and interchange, between the exoteric, or outer aspects, and the esoteric, or inner aspects, of that great world religion. I hope to abstract and offer, as it were, both its substance and its present-day applications in simple terms that appeal simultaneously to the mind, the heart, and the will. Therefore, this volume will explore and analyze the "further aspects of living and practical Christianity" announced at the end of the first volume.

The two volumes are designed to be read and studied independently. Yet the reader should bear in mind that each volume forms an integral and complementary part of the other, just as each chapter is an independent unit that sheds further light on and complements the others. The cumulative impact of all chapters and both volumes form a whole which is greater than the sum of its parts! Moreover, as the distinctive approach used here is based far more upon direct personal experience and vision than upon scholarship or rational analysis, reading both volumes together will make each one far more meaningful, love-provoking, and action-generating than reading either alone.

Together, *Divine Light and Fire* and *Divine Light and Love* represent the mature fruits of the spiritual quest of a lifetime—my own! At the very least, they represent the objective and concrete fulfillment of my earliest dreams and visions, of my highest aspirations, and of over thirty-five years of painstaking research, careful experimentation, and meaningful personal development. While there is a close connection with one religion, Christianity, and with one of the major traditions within this religion, Catholicism (as I use its language and rituals), this book does not deal primarily with religion, not even with a catholic or universal religion. What it deals with, rather, is *human and spiritual growth, personal and collective initiation, the qualitative expansion of human consciousness and the dawning of spiritual consciousness.* As such, it is truly universal and experiential in nature and purpose, and can be grasped in its substance and applied in daily life by *any interested person of good will* who is willing to submit to its discipline of personal training, purification, and consecration.

This work describes a simple, practical, efficacious and safe *Path of Initiation* for the modern man and woman who feel a deep yearning for something more than material, social, or professional achievements; who feel the sacred Fire awakening within their hearts; and who aspire to what is real, lasting, and highest in life. As such, it has far more in common with the "Primordial Tradition," the "*philosophia perennis,*" "the ageless wisdom," or the true "*Theos-Sophia*" (the Wisdom of God), than it has with organized Christianity . . . even though it does draw upon and utilizes the language, rituals, and spiritual structure carried forth, and transmitted through the centuries, by the Orthodox and Catholic Christian traditions! Paradoxically, it suggests that original, or early, Christianity (before Constantine made it the state religion of the Roman Empire in the fourth century) was precisely this "universal brotherhood and sisterhood" and Path of Initiation . . . and not an organized religion at all.

Manifestly, *Divine Light and Fire* emphasizes and works with the ritualistic and ceremonial approach I call the "yoga of the West." But I would argue that today, this ritualistic and ceremonial approach is essential also for the seekers of the Eastern tradition who live in large and polluted cities where it becomes more and more important to be able to switch on and off one's higher receptivities and levels of consciousness. This work looks for and tries to articulate the simplest and most effective way of developing a comprehensive "philosophy of life" and of embodying an "integral art of living" (insofar as I am able to comprehend and articulate these at this point in my life). It looks for and finds its basic tools and instruments in the images, symbols, myths, and rituals of Catholic Christianity, but *interpreted in a spiritual way.*

The implicit thesis, or central assumption, of this work, is that, *on the higher levels of consciousness and being,* in the Communion of Saints, there is but One religion, one way to unite with the spiritual Self and with Ultimate Reality, both *within* and *without*: The Religion of the Saints, Sages, and Initiates, the "Inner Church," the "Brotherhood of the Rosy-Cross" which is not now and has never been fully incarnated or institutionalized in this world. In this world there are many "embodied" and "institutionalized" religions, which correspond to different levels of evolution, consciousness, and being and which express different personal values, experiences, and emphases. But, insofar as I have been able to experience them, they all lead, "like the rays of a circle to the point in the center," to the One Religion; which, for lack of a better term, I call the "Religion of the Holy Spirit." This dimension of religion has always existed and can be found at the mystical core of all authentic religions and sacred traditions, yet it transcends them. It is none other than the direct vision and personal experience of the most profound teachings of religion and of its crowning objective: *conscious union with God.* This is why this volume is dedicated to the United Nations and to all those who labor within and without its "walls" to realize its magnificent ideal of a peaceful and united world.

In this work, I have linked together and given a voice to essential elements of both my personal biography and my human, intellectual, and spiritual experiences and realizations up to now. Each chapter of *Divine Light and Love* can be and has been used independently as core material for a lecture or a workshop. But taken as a whole, this book provides an integrated and coherent (but dynamic and open) theoretical framework or "philosophy" and a practical discipline to activate one's intuition, accelerate consciously one's evolution, and achieve spiritual consciousness. A person who achieves this becomes a truly autonomous being, inner-guided and spirit-driven, no longer dependent upon external or foreign structures and experts, and thus truly able to be and express all that he or she is! It is at this point that the true *joie de vivre,* our greatest and most living form of thanksgiving and gratitude to our Heavenly Father and Mother, can be realized—and radiated to others. I hope this work will be thought-provoking, heart-stirring, and action-encouraging for practicing Catholics and formal Christians. But it can equally contribute practically and meaningfully to persons of other religions or of no religion at all, as it aims at a "spiritual science" based on direct and personal *observation* and *experience*. Certainly, the last thing that this work would attempt to do is to proselytize or seek to convert persons from one religion to another!

Divine Light and Fire explicitly stated both a quest and methods for a personal adventure in the field of religion (Catholic and Orthodox Christianity in particular) as well as in the field of personal growth and spiritual awakening. Thus, it began by describing the age in which we live—its dangers and opportunities, and its conception of the "spiritual quest." It moved on to analyze several aspects of the Christian tradition from the spiritual or esoteric point of view. Drawing from my own studies and experiences, I examined what this tradition is, where it might be going, and what potential contributions it could make to the coming age. Specifically, I looked at what the Christian Church, or Temple, really is, and how it can best be used for expanding one's consciousness, raising one's vibrations, and unfolding spiritual consciousness. I explained the "exoteric" and the "esoteric" aspects of religion and how they can be *complementary* rather than *opposed* to each other. I described the language of religion, and how it differs from the language of everyday speech and the language of science. I explained how the language of religion can be used for self-actualization and spiritual purposes to make the images, symbols, and rituals of *any tradition* speak to us again and reveal their mysteries and treasures. I especially looked at the "Seven Sacraments" of the Catholic traditions as they related to our psychospiritual Centers and to the various levels of Initiation—at how they can be properly understood and used for human and spiritual growth and Self-realization. My aim is not to impose my own views on others, but rather to stimulate readers to do their own work to achieve their own authentic esoteric realization and synthesis,—to create the Soul-Sculpture where each person is both the artist and the work of art. This is the point at which *Divine Light and Fire* ended, giving its readers an understanding of the theoretical implications and the practical applications of living and esoteric Christianity good enough to enable them to put these to work in their own lives.

The present volume continues this quest and work. It analyzes from the esoteric viewpoint a series of interrelated topics that both complement each other and add further "light" to the first volume, just as the subjects covered in the first volume can do the same for the second volume. Since what is said about Christianity also applies to and can shed further on "light" and elicit more "respect" for the other valid religions and traditions, it begins with an "exoteric-esoteric" investigation of the Roman Catholic Mass, showing, briefly, what it is and how it can be used for *spiritual purposes.* This will serve as a recapitulation and a practical synthesis and application of the substance of the first volume.

It continues by explaining what I call the "vertical axis of human consciousness" and its implications. I compare a human being to a sky-scraper with one hundred floors, each of which corresponds to a qualitatively different level of consciousness and being wherein "reality" is perceived and conceived in a different way. Realizing this can help one be tolerant and understanding of people who are on "different floors" and who use different approaches, methods, religions, and levels of the same religion. Then, I will describe a "journey to the Outer Church leading to the Inner Church" with the appropriate symbolism, correspondences, and exercises designed to lead the seeker to a temporary but *conscious* communion with the Christ within, the Divine Spark. Next will come an analysis of Prayer—its nature, functions, psychospiritual mechanisms, and purpose. This will lead to a discussion of the spiritual nature and contributions of a "pilgrimage" in the world and, analogically, within one's own consciousness. Following this, I will look at "Health and Disease", "Sin and Salvation" in the present and the coming age. Finally, I will explore the nature of the "Priest" to the "Initiate" in the coming Era.

In this volume, I also include three appendixes: the first dealing with the Tree of Life and the psychospiritual Centers; the second exploring in greater detail the core psychospiritual processes of human consciousness I call the "Muscles of Human Consciousness;" and the last outlining and analyzing the "core fragments" of a "comprehensive philosophy of life" and of an "integral art of living", specifically designed for our present and coming age, for modern men and women who want to live Life at its fullest, most conscious and joyful level. And this not so that earnest readers and seekers might copy it or make it "their own," but to inspire and motivate them to *develop* their own, unique and personal model.

As the author of this book, I am very concerned with hearing from my readers and creating a dialogue with them insofar as this is humanly possible, to discuss their reactions to and results from using the ideas in this work, and to compare their experiences and conclusions with those of the persons actively involved in groups with me; for the Quest ever goes on in this world, from level to level, from realization to realization, and from Wonder to Wonder—until we shall all meet in the spiritual worlds, the Inner Church, or the Communion of Saints.

CHAPTER ONE

The Roman Catholic Mass: A Contemporary Esoteric Experience

Of all contemporary Christian services, the Roman Catholic Mass is perhaps the best known and, from a practical view, the most easily available; but it is also "practical" in a higher sense, as a spiritual practice, a way to achieve that spiritual interaction, or Communion, with the Divine Spark, with God, which is the ultimate objective of all authentic spiritual work. Of all the many and fast-proliferating psychospiritual exercises available to the modern spiritual seeker, this is the simplest, yet most essential; the most practical yet deeply and profoundly effective. Besides being the best known, it is also able to realize the highest and most important spiritual goal—union with God, a temporary connection with, and immersion in, the very Source and Essence of all Life, Love and Wisdom. It entails an increasingly conscious, full and intense "transfusion and suffusion" with the Divine Light, Fire, and Life of the Christ within. Its purpose is that He may become "our Lord," the center and ruling principle of our consciousness and behavior as He objectively is without, the Lord of all Creation. This can only occur if we have a minimal understanding of the Mass and its deeper psychodynamics and purpose, and that we live it with all the Faith we are capable of mustering while we move through it. Speaking of the Mass, Evelyn Underhill states:

> Into [the Mass] the worshiping instinct of generations has poured itself; and bit by bit there has been added to the Christian ritual pattern all those fundamental responses to God which are latent in the religious

soul. At last, in the fully developed liturgy, the whole drama of creation and redemption—God's loving movement toward man, and man's response in Christ—is recapitulated; and all the implications which lay hidden in its small origins, the grain of wheat which was flung into the field of the world, are brought to maturity.[1]

Any authentic spiritual exercise requires our total participation and involvement—the full dedication, purification, and consecration of our will, mind, and love—for what it is is perceived according to our level of consciousness. It also helps to gain an understanding of the nature and use of images, symbols, myths, and rituals as the "language of the Deep Mind." This language is understood by the unconscious, subconscious, and superconscious mind; it is the language that since ancient times has been used by the sacred traditions. This language is symbolic and analogical, and operates as a function of our level of consciousness, with as many different meanings, implications, and applications as there are different levels of consciousness. Thus, it can reveal, as well as veil, many mysteries and truths, and is therefore very different from the descriptive language of everyday speech or the analytical language of conventional science. Yet, there is a place here as well for a true spiritual science in learning, training, and coordinating the faculties of human consciousness; in particular, concentration, meditation, visualization, and invocation and evocation.

The Catholic Mass, like most sacred spiritual practices, is subdivided into three basic parts:

Roman Catholic Mass	*Orthodox Liturgy*	*Spiritual Work*
A. Introductory Rites	The Office of Prothesis	Purification
B. The Liturgy of the Word	The Liturgy of the Catechumens	Consecration
C. The Liturgy of the Eucharist	The Liturgy of the Faithful	Unification

The prayers and rituals of the Mass can be experienced using the methods which I described in *The Nature and Use of Ritual for Spiritual Achievement*,[2] that is, meditation, contemplation, and theurgy. In essence, this means to concentrate and meditate, regularly and repeatedly, upon every core symbol, every petition, and, then upon the whole prayer, petition, or ritual. And, finally, to approach the whole theurgically. Let us see what this means.

The Introductory Rites

The Entrance Song is spoken or sung while all stand. In a solemn Mass (which is mostly sung), the Priest with his assistants walk down the center aisle, perhaps with the choir leading the way. The Priest bows to the altar, then faces the people.

Preparing to listen to the Word of God and to celebrate the Eucharist, the Priest makes the Sign of the Cross over the congregation, saying: "In the Name of the Father, and of the Son, and of the Holy Spirit." The worshipers should acknowledge this by tracing three times the same Sign of the Cross over themselves. This awakens the Head Center, as a calling to and activation of the Divine Light ("In the Name of the Father") in the mental, astral, and etheric bodies respectively; then is awakened the Heart Center, calling and activating the Divine Fire ("In the Name of the Son") in these higher bodies; finally, this awakens the Shoulder Centers, calling and activating the Divine Vital, Creative, and Vivifying Energies ("In the Name of the Holy Spirit") in the higher bodies. There are, of course many facets and correspondences, that can rise in the heart, mind, and soul, with respect to the Cross as one's conscious involvement grows.[3] (I have written in greater detail, in a chapter on the Sign of the Cross, in *The Nature and Use of Ritual for Spiritual Attainment,* to which I refer the reader once again.)

The Sign of the Cross, in what it calls to mind and in all the ways that we can take this sign within us and awaken it in us, is a natural point of entry into the spiritual work about to begin. It is a sign that we are entering another sphere, beyond the purely mundane. Yet we bring that which our time carries with it, the burden of much conflict, confusion, and pollution on all levels, that which "clogs" our centers of perception and expression, that which has put our psyches to sleep. This sign "lights up" our awareness and knowledge, our feeling and love, our creative energies, and thus initiates the purification and consecration that follows.

> Priest: "The grace of our Lord Jesus Christ and the love of God and the fellowship of the Holy Spirit be with you all."
> People: "And also with you."

This is a symbolic, yet actual, projection of the Divine Light, Fire, and Life upon the faithful, whose psychospiritual Centers have been awakened by the previous Sign of the Cross. Thus, one should cross oneself three times, experiencing the mental, emotional, and vital transformations, or *metanoia*, that this ritual brings about in one's own consciousness and project them back to the Priest. This procedure establishes a "living and dynamic circuit" between the Priest and the faithful. In terms of the Tree of Life, this means bringing through the Energies, Vibrations, and Materials of Kether, Chockmah, and Binah to Chesed, Geburah, and Tipphereth to make the Superconscious conscious. (In your consciousness and Aura, the Priest can be seen, as a first stage, to represent your conscious ego and its three essential faculties—thinking, feeling, and willing—with the altar, Tipphereth, as your Heart Center; then, what the Priest does at the altar can be mirrored in your own heart.)

> Priest: "The Grace and Peace of God the Father and the Lord Jesus Christ be with you."
> People: "Blessed be God, the Father of our Lord Jesus Christ" or "And also with you."

Grace, what is grace? (One must be granted the grace to explain it!) Surely, it is a gift of God, the gift of His Life to us. It provokes us to action; we know this in how it is often used, the "grace to" do something, that one may be granted that Spiritual Energy; here we can call to mind what we may be inspired to bring to the Mass now as it begins: we can ask for the grace to be fully present. It also recognizes that the grace of the Kingdom of God is already present, within and without, would we but realize it.

Peace is another gift, that which "passeth all understanding;" but it is also a crucial task, very much so in our time, within and without. Within, from an esoteric view, this can mean the harmonious alignment and "aliveness" of all our higher bodies together with our physical body, the opened and balanced functioning of our Centers, and all the spiritual faculties we have spoken of throughout this work. With these words, the Priest blesses us, once again, projecting Energy and Light to the faithful, awakening us, filling us with these, raising and reorganizing our consciousness around the Consciousness and Will of the Christ. And these Energies are, again, sent back to the Priest to further activate the "exchanges:" the horizontal exchanges between the Priest and the faithful and the vertical exchanges between the Superconscious and the conscious.

A *blessing*, moreover, is a Light-extension and an Energy-projection from a higher to a lower source to vivify and activate the latter.

> Priest: "The Lord be with you."
> People: "And also with you."

At the conclusion of the previous ritual, the worshiper should begin to feel and experience the Presence, Consciousness, and Activity of the Christ, both within himself and in the Temple.

The Penitential Rite

> Priest: "My brothers and sisters, to prepare ourselves to celebrate the sacred mysteries, let us call to mind our sins."
> All: "I confess to Almighty God, and to you, my brothers and sisters, that I have sinned through my own fault in what I have done and what I have failed to do; and I ask Blessed Mary, ever Virgin, all the Angels and Saints, and you, my brothers and sisters, to pray for me to the Lord our God."

This is one of the few passages of the Mass which is written in a simple descriptive language rather than in the usual symbolic, archetypal, and analogical one. A few things can be noted; that this is addressed to Almighty God, to whom the sacrifice of the Mass is offered; that the community, the family of God, with the Priest united as a brother among brothers and sisters is implicit; the Blessed Mother is invoked, the Mother of this family, and the community of Saints and Angels. Mary has many titles in the

Catholic tradition and it is significant that here she is invoked as "ever Virgin" in this, the purification part of the service.

Two basic esoteric points should, however, be emphasized. Firstly, that the worshiper should go through his or her own personal and internal Confession Rite with as much attention, concentration, awareness, and feeling as he or she can muster, going through a full and honest examination of his or her conscience. In this we can experience, too, what the consequences of sin have been and are in our lives and consciousnesses, both in their vertical and horizontal dimensionalities. Violations of universal laws are both vertical and horizontal, blocking and distorting our conscious exchanges with the Christ within (thinking, feeling, and willing), also with the Celestial Hierarchies—the Angelic Orders, Saints, the departed—and with other human beings, as well as with animals, plants, and the earth.

Thus, by violating cosmic laws, God's Laws, we cut ourselves off, severing the flow of Life and Consciousness both vertically and horizontally on many levels of our being, as well as among ourselves, God, other human beings, and nature. It is this inner and outer harmony or "chain of life" that is to now be restored, by the Grace of God.

Priest: "Lord, we have sinned against You: Lord, have mercy."
People: "Lord, have mercy."
Priest: "Lord, show us Your Mercy and Love."
People: "And grant us Your Salvation."

This passage reinforces the former passage in recognizing that we have all sinned, in countless ways, both consciously and unconsciously, by omission and commission, and thus that we all need mercy and salvation. In violating universal laws, God's Laws, in sinning, we act against God as He is within us as the Self, the Divine Spark, and as the Absolute and Almighty Creator. In what we do unto others (and unto all created nature) we do unto Him, thus unto Him in us, unto ourselves. Bearing the consequences in the esoteric tradition has the added dimension that, later on, we will be compelled to go through and experience on a higher plane of existence what we have done to others as they experienced it.

When we think, feel, will, speak, and act in ways that break the inner harmony of Being, we immediately pass to a lower state of consciousness and being which affects our perceptions, thoughts, feelings, and choices. We literally pass from Life to death, or from consciousness to unconsciousness, in breaking the "Great Chain of Being." The result of this is that we become estranged from the Source and Essence of Life, Love, and Wisdom, and from who we really are, and that we are "lost" and in great need of salvation or reconnection.

In the esoteric tradition, "mercy," having as it does three Hebrew roots, is also a plurality; specifically, of the Spiritual Energies, Light, Fire, and Life and the consciousness of the Supernals (Kether, Chockmah, and Binah), manifesting itself through the three highest psychospiritual Centers in our Tree of Life, which can realign our being with the Christ. Without this "connection," we find ourselves thrown into the sphere of death, unconsciousness, separation, loneliness, and suffering.

Priest: "Lord, have mercy." People: "Lord, have mercy."
Priest: "Christ, have mercy." People: "Christ, have mercy."
Priest: "Lord, have mercy." People: "Lord have mercy."

This is the final repetition and reinforcement of the former ritual where mercy, technically speaking, is the down-pouring of Spiritual Energies (Light, Fire, and Life) from the Supernals (Kether, Chockmah, and Binah) through Chesed, to the rest of the Tree of Life. Also, the threefold repetition applies here, as elsewhere, to the three main "energy bodies" of the personality—the mental, the emotional, and the vital.

Priest: "May Almighty God have mercy on us, forgive us our sins, and bring us to everlasting Life."

This is the Absolution of the Penitential Rite, which can also be repeated three times by the worshiper, with all the Faith he or she can muster. We can also recall that Absolution is associated with "Netzach," the Left Hip Center and the restoration of the inner and outer harmony of the Great Chain of Being.

The Gloria (sung by all): "Glory to God in the highest, and peace to his people on earth. Lord God, Heavenly King, Almighty God and Father, we worship you, we give you thanks, we praise you for your glory.

Lord Jesus Christ, only Son of the Father, Lord God, Lamb of God, you take away the sins of the world: Have mercy on us; you are seated at the right hand of the Father: receive our prayer. For you alone are the Holy One, you alone are the Lord, you alone are the Most High, Jesus Christ, with the Holy Spirit, in the glory of God the Father. Amen."

Glory is that which belongs to God alone, the power, majesty, honor, and radiance which are His alone. Since Old Testament times, His Glory has been experienced, often associated with awesome natural occurrences; but in Jesus Christ, in the unity of the Cross and the Resurrection is glory revealed in a love stronger than all sin and death, a glorious love greater than which it is impossible to conceive. "Glory to God in the highest," esoterically speaking, is to fill with the Light and Life (Glory) our own Head Center, "Kether," represented by a Sphere of dazzling White Light, slightly larger than our physical head, slightly higher, yet interpenetrating it, so as to contact it and activate it consciously. Thus, to open ourselves to God's Glory is to empty ourselves, that He may pour His Spirit, His Light into us, as water into an empty cup. "Peace to his people on earth" is this Light, then, flowing throughout ourselves, connecting the Divine Spark with all our "bodies," Centers, and faculties, aligning our being and consciousness with His Lordship, so that we may more fully give to God glory in the world through our actions and deeds. To worship God the Father, who is our Heavenly King, to give Him thanks and praise Him for His Glory is to pour forth all our attention and energies, love and feelings, thoughts and consciousness upon Him; to express all the gratitude we can generate for His Love and Gifts—as well as to light up our psychospiritual Head Center, activate it and integrate it as the unifying and integrating principle of our consciousness and behavior.

The next passage can again awaken in our consciousness the realization that it is He who "takes away our sins," heals us, makes us whole, and enables us truly to be ourselves and to express ourselves, and thus to fulfill His and our purposes in this world. The Mercy of the Lord is not only a forgiveness for our sins, it is also an expression of His Light and Energies. This can be especially perceived, according to esoteric tradition, through our Left

Shoulder Center, "Chesed," which can in turn light, activate, and coordinate our Tree of Life, consciousness, and being. "Seated" at the right hand of the Father, is Christ, but He is within us as the Divine Spark, of whom we attempt to be always conscious as the ruling and unifying principle of our life and being. For it is the Inner Lord and Master who alone should be our "Guiding Principle," and not the many entities, energies, and functions of our consciousness. Jesus Christ achieved and incarnated this realization, thus paving the way for us to do the same—in that way He is the Divine Human Prototype and Archetype, or model. "Amen" means "so be it," let it be achieved and realized, according to Thy Will.

The Gloria brings the first part of the Mass, the Introductory and Penitential Rites, to a close. The aims and purposes are many in terms of the spiritual preparation that occurs on many levels. It is not our purpose here fully to delineate all aspects, implications, and consequences of these rites. With respect to how these can indeed become more fully manifest in the consciousness of the worshiper, using the approaches we have suggested throughout, we can briefly highlight two processes:

a. These rites can enable the worshipers to change their level of consciousness and attention from our normal state of extraversion in the external, physical world to one of introversion, to that of our inner consciousness and its various inner states and changes. Our own internal deepening then allows us to more fully participate in the dynamic exchanges between inner and outer; we do not become less conscious of the external, but can enter with new life into it once we have begun to plumb these depths within ourselves.

b. A cleansing, purification, and transformation of ourselves (and, as we have seen, the effects extend far out from ourselves to others, to the community, to the world) can take place in our consciousness, in our centers of awareness, in our higher bodies; this is not only a conscious cleansing but works as well on the subconscious and even unconscious planes, as we prepare to be in the best possible inner state for the next part of the Mass, the "Liturgy of the Word," a phase of personal consecration.

The Liturgy of the Word

The second phase of the Mass begins with a first and second reading of the Scriptures together with a responsorial psalm. These readings have as their purpose to focus the mind, heart, and attention of the worshipers upon selected passages of the Scriptures that fit into the liturgical calendar. These readings can provide the imagination and the intuition of the worshipers with specific archetypal images and events which can bring into their fields of consciousness certain materials, energies, and vibrations that awaken their psyches and redirect their consciousness to the spiritual dimension of their being. The Bible speaks directly to this consciousness in the living language of symbolic and analogic reality, beyond the duality that modern conception imposes on sign and reality. It is the great story of the relationship of God to man, as God has revealed Himself to man through history, through timeless myth and symbol and through Jesus Christ; and it is also our very own spiritual and evolutionary autobiography. Thus, each person can recognize himself or herself, in the two passages that are read and experienced at whatever level of consciousness or degree of human experience we have.

At the end of the First Reading (for which all sit), the reader says: "This is the Word of the Lord." And the people respond: "Thanks be to God." Then, in the solemn Mass, a responsorial Psalm is sung. The Psalms are of exquisite beauty, and, as they often follow the boldness and clarity of the Apostle Paul in the first reading, they provide a spiritual counterpoint in their poetic and lyrical virtuosity. It can also be a moment of great poignancy and love for all, which has roots in the people of Israel and their inspiring example of faith. One can experience how singing here awakens, lifts, and blends the collective consciousness of all present, attuning them one to the other.

At the end of the second reading (all are still seated), the reader says: "This is the Word of the Lord." And the people respond: "Thanks be to God." Then the Alleluia is sung, interspersed with a verse, as all rise to their feet. (Like the Gloria, the Alleluia is not sung during Lent.)

Then the Gospel passage for the day is read while all stand. The priest or deacon says: "The Lord be with you" and the people answer, "And also with you." The priest or deacon says: "A reading of the Holy Gospel according to N." And the people answer: "Glory to You, Lord." At the end of the Gospel, the priest or deacon says, again: "This is the Gospel of the Lord." And the people answer: "Praise to You, Lord Jesus Christ."

As are all universal messages, the Gospels are written in symbolic, archetypal language. And to reach all people, each on his or her individual level of consciousness and being, they are written in the language of the Four Elements: Earth for physical-practical consciousness, Water for emotional consciousness, Air for mental consciousness, and Fire for spiritual consciousness. This is why the Four Evangelists have the symbols of the Four Cardinal Signs of the Zodiac—the bull, Taurus; the man, Aquarius; the lion, Leo; and the eagle, Scorpio: So that they can appeal and be meaningful to the practical person, the artist, the intellectual, and the intuitive or mystical person.

The Four Gospels tell the Life and Teachings of Jesus Christ, the Lord. Thus, symbolically, they also represent the biography and saga—the incarnation, crucifixion, resurrection, and ascension—of the Christ within, of the Divine Spark, the true but as yet unknown Self of every human being. In the Gospels, therefore, what a student of the Mysteries or an Initiate finds is his or her own biography and personal story with all the essential stages, trials, and crises of their becoming and spiritual enlightenment. It is up to us—to each one of us—to become aware and incarnate, and to live that particular event which best corresponds to our level of consciousness, our present evolutionary phase, our existential situation and crisis. By recalling and inwardly making these archetypal events "come alive" and reliving them, we tune into the Christ within and harmonize our own consciousness with His while He is also ever seeking to embrace us with the fullness of His Love. And we bridge, as it were, the conscious with the superconscious, the human with the spiritual Self; we enable Him to be resurrected *in our very own consciousness.* This is the esoteric Christian way of reconsecrating ourselves and of lighting up all of the psychospiritual Centers in our own Tree of Life.

Then, comes the Profession of Faith, the Creed.[4] The etymological roots of "creed" can be traced back through the Latin *credo*, itself from *cor* (the heart) and the verb *platia* to place. Thus "creed" implies putting one's heart into something or someone. There is a long and complex (and ongoing) history of creeds in Christianity; St. Augustine referred to a creed as a *symbolum fidei* (symbol of faith) and Tertullian to a "rule of faith." Initially it was part of the baptismal rite, but was later to become part of the Eucharistic liturgy.

From an esoteric point of view, the Creed signifies that we can unite in spirit with all Christians—despite what externally continues to divide the different confessions—in the faith that we shall one day realize the One Church. This spirit of union within is sure to proceed outwardly to be then realized in the world, for awakened in us through the living symbols and archetypes of the Creed are the powers of the Holy Trinity: the Father Almighty who awakens in us Divine Wisdom; His only beloved Son, our Lord Jesus Christ who awakens in us Divine Love; and the Holy Spirit, the Giver of Life, which awakens in us Divine Creative Energies. Of course, there are many more attributes of the Holy Trinity that can be mentioned here—more, indeed, than can be mentioned at all—but the interior experience of the Holy Trinity united with the Church, which within us is known esoterically as the Human Soul, can be the experience of these attributes, among others. We can feel this as the final consecration of our consciousness and being for the coming Communion and Unification of the third and final part of the Mass.

It is important to remember the inner sequence of the connection between Heaven and Earth, of how we may seek the "Word become Flesh" as a living reality in our human nature: First, we must become aware of and grasp cognitively what is being said by the priest at the altar. Then we can repeat and affirm that in our own heart. Then we must feel it, experience it emotionally in our own being. If we will live it in our own being and lives, we can hope to be worthy of the grace to become it, incarnate it, and thus to fully realize it, if that is God's will.

This part ends with General Intercessions, which are prayers offered by the Priest or the people, dealing normally with specific liturgical or external events for which all are urged to pray. Having gone through the preparatory phases of personal purification and consecration, we are now ready for the final and culminating part of the Mass, the liturgy of the Eucharist, Communion, or Unification.

The Liturgy of the Eucharist

The Preparation of the Gifts

While the altar is being prepared and the gifts of the people are brought forward, we can feel how these gifts are what we are all bringing to offer to God: our hearts, minds, wills, talents, initiatives, and energies, our very best in what we are, feel, create, and do. In esoteric terms, the Gifts correspond to the auras or Energy Bodies and the psychospiritual Centers, in particular the Hearts, the Minds, and the Wills of the worshipers. These will now be suffused and transformed by Christ, we can experience here His Divine Light and Fire descend as the transformation of these gifts begins. A song is then sung by the congregation while the Priest says the following prayers:

> Priest: "Blessed are You, Lord, God of Creation. Through Your goodness we have this Bread to offer, which the earth has given and human hands have made. It will become for us the Bread of Life."
> People: "Blessed be God for ever."

Is it not strange to bless God, for creatures to bless the Creator? But here "Blessed be God" means we are offering praise and thanks to God for all we have to offer: He has blessed us with them and we in turn bless Him by worship, service, praise, and thanksgiving. It is a means of communication, recognizing a two-way exchange of love. Esoterically speaking, a blessing is a Light-projection and Energy-extension from one source to another. Here in particular, we can focus our thought, feeling, and attention on the psychospiritual Head Center to establish a "circuit" with Him. The "Bread of Life" is Jesus Christ as the Divine Light of all worlds, while the physical bread is to be, mysteriously, His embodiment in the material world. Here, therefore, Heaven and Earth, the Divine Light and physical bread, are joined and connected together so that the physical bread now becomes the "channel" or "conductor" for the spiritual Light of the Self. Included in the people's response is a symbolic way of representing every part, level, and facet of our being (all the bodies, centers, and faculties of our little Kingdom) which link up and enter into a living and conscious connection with the Divine Spark and its Light and Power.

Priest: "Blessed are You, Lord of all creation. Through Your goodness we have this wine to offer, fruit of the vine and work of human hands. It will become our spiritual drink."
People: "Blessed be God forever."

The same process is repeated here but with the focus this time being on the wine, a symbol of Love. The "wine" we have to offer is human love, fruit of the earth and of human energies, just as He offers His Love in His new covenant in His Blood, the cup He offers for us and to us. Into this wine and human love pours forth the *Divine Fire* into our Heart Center; the "spiritual drink" is thus experienced as Divine Fire, which from the spiritual worlds, enters into the wine in the physical world. Here, through the second blessing, the spiritual Wine and the physical wine are united so that the latter can become, mysteriously, the former, vivifying us. Heaven and Earth, the Head and the Heart, are now joined so that, together as the vertical Male and Female Principles, they may engender the divine Creative Energies, the Divine Will linked to the human will, manifesting through a genuine and living creativity the real expression of the Holy Spirit.

Thus it is that we can "bless God" with all our thoughts, feelings, and attention and become suffused and permeated by His Divine Light, Fire, and Creative Energies, in a living and evermore conscious circuit of Life. Here, Heaven and Earth, Male and Female, Supraversion and Infraversion, Extraversion and Introversion, Superconscious and Conscious—Man and God—can thus be connected and commune one with the other.

Priest: "Pray, brethren, that our sacrifice may be acceptable to God, the Almighty Father."
People: "May the Lord accept the sacrifice at our hands for the praise and glory of His Name, for our good, and the good of all His Church."

This is the Prayer over the Gifts. Prayer always involves an "alchemy of life," as the transformation of human consciousness, energies and vibrations felt in response to the presence of God. It is a gift of "spiritual interaction" with Him which, esoterically, we can see as exchanges between the field of consciousness and the Superconscious, the human and the Spiritual Self. For most people, unfortunately, it yet remains either an unconscious mechanical or a purely intellectual process, but it can increasingly become a conscious, vivifying, and transforming act, lived with heart and mind, soul and spirit, whether in petition, thanksgiving, atonement, or adoration.

A "sacrifice" ("making holy or sacred") involves the twin processes of emptying something and then filling it; that is, exchanging something on one plane for something else on another plane; to dying or emptying oneself on one level, to be reborn or refilled on another level. Thus, it necessarily involves the opposites of pain and joy, of agony and ecstasy. Here, the sacrifice we offer includes all of our human knowledge, love, and will (thinking, feeling, and willing) in hope and faith that Christ will transform them into Divine Wisdom, Love and Will, thereby uniting us with Him. It is when we open ourselves, empty ourselves, give of ourselves, that the spiritual Energies can conduct their psychospiritual alchemy.

Thus the Priest prays that all we are, can feel, or do is "acceptable" (that is, made capable of "blending with" the Light, Fire, and Life of the Divine Spark which is Christ within us), so that this circuit, within and without, is opened and made ready for the transformation; such is the substructure or foundation of Communion and Union.

When the "people" respond, this refers to everyone present physically in the Church at the time of the Mass. There is another sense, a microcosmic sense of "people," which refers to the world within, the "Little Kingdom" or the "Human Temple"; thus, affirmations in this and all responses of the people are also affirmations throughout our inner domain, throughout all of our higher bodies, in each of our centers of awareness, across the topography of this inner "Kingdom."

"For the praise and glory of His Name" reminds us that gratitude is one of the basic attitudes and experiences of soul, which in our lives opens the gates leading to Communion with God, within and without. As the Mass is in itself a microcosm, in the sense of a compact living symbol of our lives, we can ask here what in our lives is not done "for the praise and glory of His Name?" It is the purpose of the sacrifice of the Mass to render this glory and praise unto God, as it is too the purpose of human life. But we ask in the Prayer over the Gifts that God return to us what is good for us, which He alone knows that is, Faith that we may be worthy of His Light, Fire, and Life within, to radiate them wherever we are.

The Eucharistic Prayer

Priest: "The Lord be with you."
People: "And also with you."
Priest: "Lift up your hearts."
People: "We lift them up to the Lord."
Priest: "Let us give thanks to the Lord our God."
People: "It is right to give Him thanks and praise."

These words of the Preface again emphasize the exchange that is now being established by the humble supplication of all present to the Lord, as He now draws closer to us, as we to Him. All within us, the conscious ego united with all the other aspects and facets of our being, is united in one "lifting up" of our hearts—our thinking heart, our feeling heart, and our willing heart—as without "We" are united in lifting up likewise our communal hearts.

The communion that is being prepared here, within and without, is also a profound recognition of community. In recognizing the Divine Spark in another human being, we also awaken it and activate it in ourselves; and the wheel turns as well the other way, knowing it in ourselves, we recognize it in others, as it is only the Divine within that can recognize the Divine without. And it is the Heart Center we lift up into which the Divine Spark has to descend (that is, to "lower" or translate His vibrations) in order for our human selves, our conscious egos, to become aware of Him. Once we do become aware of Him, and increasingly as we become more aware, it will seem "right to give Him praise and thanks."

Priest: "Father, it is our duty and our salvation, always and everywhere, to give you thanks through your beloved Son, Jesus Christ. He is the

Word through whom you made the universe, the Savior you sent to redeem us. By the power of the Holy Spirit he took flesh and was born of the Virgin Mary. For our sake he opened his arms on the cross; he put an end to death and revealed the resurrection. In this he fulfilled your will and won for you a holy people. And so we join the angels and the saints in proclaiming your glory as we say:"
All: "Holy, holy, Lord, God of power and might, heaven and earth are full of your glory. Hosanna in the highest. Blessed is he who comes in the Name of the Lord. Hosanna in the highest."

As we lift up our hearts, so are we lifted up; and there is at this moment a sense of the universal community, the community of all beings who worship at the Throne of God. We recognize ourselves as spiritual beings, translated to the spiritual world (which is present at all times) along with the spheres of angels and saints, all proclaiming what now fills these spheres.

If our hearts are offered up, lifted up, and we with them, we are brought within, translated to another level, into a cosmic sense of community of worshipers. In the radiant golden sphere of Light and Majesty that surrounds the Throne of God, we stand and raise our voices each as a one voice among the multitude of heavenly spirits, but we each have our place in this heavenly choir: we have not lost, in this ineffable bliss, but further gained our Selfhood in surrendering it in praise.

The span of religious reference [of the Eucharist] has been so widened and the supernatural significance so deepened by the ever-growing experience of the living Church and the insights and meditations of the saints, that it now embraces and harmonizes the most simple and most abstract spiritual experiences possible to men; placing them within the universal act of worship which the world, visible and invisible, offers to its Creator and Lord. [5]

After the Sanctus is sung, the people kneel. The Priest replaces the chalice on the altar and genuflects.

I. Eucharistic Prayer

Priest: "Father, You are holy indeed, and all creation rightly gives You praise. All life, all holiness comes from You through Your Son, Jesus Christ, our Lord, by the working of the Holy Spirit. From age to age

You gather a people to Yourself, so that from East to West a perfect offering may be made to the glory of Your Name. And so, Father, we bring you these Gifts. We ask You to make them holy by the power of Your Spirit that they may become the Body and Blood of your Son, our Lord Jesus Christ, at Whose command we celebrate this Eucharist.

On the night in which He was betrayed, He took bread and gave You thanks and praise. He broke the bread, gave it to His disciples, and said: Take this, all of you, and eat it: This is My Body which will be given up for you.

When supper was ended, He took the cup. Again He gave You thanks and Praise, gave the cup to His disciples, and said Take this all of you, and drink from it: this is the cup of My Blood, the Blood of the new and ever-lasting covenant. It will be shed for you and for all so that sins may be forgiven. Do this in memory of Me."

With this we reach the culminating point of the Mass. Just as the old radios and TV sets had inner bulbs that had to warm up and light up before the program could come through, so our Tree of Life and Energy bodies with their Centers have to "warm up" and "light up," that is, be cleansed and purified as well as consecrated and directed to a specific goal, before spiritual consciousness can dawn in us and we become able consciously to commune with the Christ within. Hence, everything that has taken place up to this moment has been a long preparation for what is now to take place. At this point, we have various Eucharistic Prayers that are vibrated by the Priest at the altar, which we have to repeat, feel, and experience in our very own Heart Center.

While different Eucharistic Prayers may be said by the Priest, we shall concentrate our attention and analysis upon only one, with the recognition that, with small variations, the others are *functionally* alike.

II. Eucharistic Prayer

Priest: "We come to you, Father, with praise and thanksgiving, through Jesus Christ Your Son. Through Him we ask You to accept and bless these Gifts we offer You in sacrifice. We offer them for Your holy Catholic Church, watch over it, Lord, and guide it; grant it peace and unity throughout the world. We offer them for N. our Pope, for M. our Bishop, and for all who hold and teach the catholic faith that comes to us from the Apostles."

Continuing with the exchanges of transcendental and historical, internal and external spiritual realities, we recall here what has been won for us in the Sacrifice of the Cross, and that through this sacrifice we are worthy to ask the Father to accept what we now offer, this living memorial. Connecting our consciousness to that of the Christ within, the Divine Light and Fire are now offered for our entire being, the microcosm, and for the whole Church and World, the macrocosm. When we "go to Communion," we can telepathically link ourselves to and offer our Communion for any other person we think about or invoke. Especially, we can offer it for the dead; many saints have spoken of the inestimable assistance this affords them.

> "Remember, Lord, your people, especially those for whom we now pray, N. and M. Remember all of us gathered here before You. You know how firmly we believe in You and dedicate ourselves to You. We offer You this sacrifice of praise for ourselves and for those who are dear to us. We pray to You, our living and true God, for our well being and redemption."

In this part of the Eucharistic Prayer we reconnect ourselves consciously with the Divine Spark within and with the Father God without, so that the Light, Fire, and Life thus invoked and manifested through the higher Spiritual Energies may flow into our being not only for our good, but for the good of those dear to us as well.

> "In union with the whole Church, we honor Mary, the ever virgin mother of Jesus Christ our Lord and God. We honor Joseph, her husband, the apostles and martyrs Peter and Paul . . . and all the Saints. May their merit and prayers gain us your constant help and protection. Through Christ our Lord. Amen."

Here in the Mass is the indissoluble union of the Mother and Son recognized. As she was present at the Paschal Mystery, as witness and, further that her spiritual perfection attuned her to His act, as none else was ever so united with it, she is also called the Co-Redemptrix. She was given by Christ on the Cross to His disciple, which we all are, as his mother, thus she is the Mother of the Church; she was teacher of the Apostles, to whom she confided no small part of the Divine Mysteries "which she kept in her heart." In Catholic tradition, the Church continues to be taught by the authority of the Holy Spirit, of whom she is the spouse, as the great St. Louis de Montfort describes:

> When the Holy Spirit, her Spouse, has found Mary in a soul, He flies there. He enters there in His fullness; He communicates Himself to that soul abundantly, and to the full extent to which it makes room for His spouse. Nay, one of the great reasons why the Holy Spirit does not now do startling wonders in our souls is because He does not find there sufficiently great union with His faithful and inseparable spouse.

It is well here to recall that there is an inner and an outer Church; the word, etymologically, derives from the Greek, *ekklesia,* from the verb, *ekkaleo,* "to summon." Throughout the New Testament, it corresponds closely to what in the Old Testament was known as *qahal,* the assembly of Israel convoked by God. Over the centuries, the building is seen as the symbol of this assembly, this community; but the Church is as well the Temple of the Holy Spirit, a mystery which can be experienced on many levels, not limited to any particular place or denomination, as we have seen. It is also the Mystical Body of Christ, which derives in scripture from Paul: "Now you are the body of Christ, and individually members of it." (1 Cor. 12:27) The Church is also profoundly linked, exoterically and esoterically, with the Mystery of the Trinity, and to the Old Testament Father, the divine mission of the Son, and the Holy Spirit. Thus we see that what can be experienced within is a crucial element by which each individual member of this Body, as part of the microcosm or the macrocosm, partakes of the Divine Life, but this is no divisive force, but a unifying one. It is a working towards an external world representation of what can be experienced within as union with God, the eventual union that realizes the inseparability of the inner and outer Church, esoteric and exoteric.

The same process is continued here with a double focus. The first focus is on the whole Church, both outer and inner, which is the symbol of the Virgin Mary. The outer Church is made up of all the people who have become "Living Stones" in the mystical Body of Christ, while the inner Church is our own consciousness, Energy Bodies, and Auras.

The second focus is on the people, the Martyrs, Saints, and Sages whose deeds inspire us to emulate them (in our own time and place and in our own way) and who act as "ideal models" or "points of reference," revealing the hidden potentialities and faculties of human nature. They are those spiritual beings in the spiritual world with whom we are in "communion" on the level of consciousness we have described as the "communion of saints."

> "Father, accept this offering from your whole family. Grant us Your peace in this life, save us from final damnation, and count us among those You have chosen. Through Christ our Lord. Amen."

Again, when we raise the offering, giving all our attention, energies, thoughts, and feelings now extended to include the entire human family, as well as all the aspects and facets of our own being, to the Lord on high and within us, as the Divine Spark. If we can really do this with all our heart, mind, and soul, then the unification in true Peace and Harmony will be reestablished, both within and without, in ourselves and the world, manifesting as our salvation. We are thereby saved, but also, because we are as of yet not totally conscious of that salvation, we are not saved until we have achieved that full realization. We can become increasingly conscious of our salvation (and of our eternal life) and collaborate in the process of bringing this salvation about.

> "Bless and approve our offering; make it acceptable to You, an offering in Spirit and in Truth. Let it become for us the Body and the Blood of Jesus Christ, Your only Son, our Lord. Through Jesus Christ our Lord. Amen."

We are moving closer to the "transubstantiation" of the bread and wine into the Body and Blood of Christ. A blessing, an outpouring of Divine Light, Fire, and Life, is invoked, together with a recognition and experience of what is transpiring. This can only be done with the help of the Power and Light of the Divine Spark, the spiritual Self, which is the Source and Essence of all spiritual Power within our being.

> "The day before He suffered, he took bread in His sacred hands and looking up to Heaven, to You, His almighty Father, He gave You thanks and praise. He broke the bread, gave it to His disciples, and said: Take this, all of you, and eat it: this is My Body which will be given up for you."

At the heart of the Eucharistic prayer are the Words of Power spoken in this final prayer of offering, sealing the transformational union between our offering of all we are and Christ's one great offering. With His words from the Last Supper, that one great historical sacrifice becomes present now in our being and consciousness, sacramentally, that we may make it our own. It is here that the mystery of the Eucharistic change is effected: the symbols of our gifts, the bread and wine, all that we are, "what earth has given and human hands have made," are changed by the sacrament, actually and meaningfully changed. These words bring down the Power, the spiritual Energies, the Divine Light and Fire, which will actually fill the bread and mysteriously change it into the Body of Christ. He gave us not only a sign of Himself, nor part of Himself, but Himself totally, on the Cross in history and now in the Eucharist. The totality of this self-giving corresponds to the totality of the change of bread and wine into Christ's very Body and Blood.

Repeating within the words "this is My body which will be given up for you" draws us into the mission of identifying with Him, with His Body as our body, which we can give up for Him, by the grace and power of the Holy Spirit. It makes possible and anticipates the communion, the union with Him.

> "When the supper was ended, He took the cup. And again He gave You thanks and praise, gave the cup to His disciples, and said: Take this, all of you, and drink from it: this is the cup of my Blood, the Blood of the new and everlasting covenant. It will be shed for you, and for all, so that sins may be forgiven. Do this in memory of Me."

In the Holy Blood is Life. As we drink from the cup—which can be visualized as opening our full being in devotion and reception of Divine Life—we are called as well to remember Him, the re-membering of ourselves, all the disparate members of His Body the Church, the re-membering of the one world under one God. The same process is continued: this time the wine is filled with the Divine Fire and is mysteriously changed to the Blood of Christ. The vivid visualization, the profound identification, and the intense concentration with strong devotion of the faithful assist the Higher Energies in their descent. Hence, it is most important that all persons repeat and live these words to the fullest possible extent in their own consciousness and hearts; for this is what makes Communion a conscious experience.

The Memorial Acclamation

Priest: "Let us proclaim the mystery of faith."

The people respond with one of four memorial acclamations which remind us that the Mass is a living memorial of the death and resurrection of Jesus Christ:

A. Christ has died,
Christ has risen,
Christ will come again.
B. Dying you destroyed our death,
rising you restored our life.
Lord Jesus, come in glory.
C. When we eat this bread and drink this cup,
we proclaim your death, Lord Jesus,
until you come in glory.
D. Lord, by your cross and resurrection
you have set us free.
You are the Savior of the world.

The Memorial Acclamation moves us from ineffability to effability, as it were; "Let us proclaim" is said in acknowledgement that "the God of power and might," to whom we sing Hosannas became human, offered Himself in the Divine Sacrifice of the Cross and gained for us Life and Freedom by His Crucifixion and Resurrection, and this is what we are enacting as a living memorial in the Mass. Faith, as was mentioned before, is all about sensing this ordering of events, the mysterious interconnection between the historical and the transcendent realities of past, present, and future in our relationship to God.

The esoteric meaning of the Acclamation can be seen in this way: Christ in us, in the microcosm, is the Divine Spark, the spiritual Self. In each of us, He has died and been crucified on the Cross of our being; that is, we are not, in our normal state of consciousness, consciously aware of Him and He cannot express His Attributes through our consciousness and behavior. Christ has risen in the historical Jesus, thus prefiguring, as archetype and prototype, that He will also rise in us. "Christ will come again" has then the meaning that He will become conscious in our beings when we awaken as new creations: "if anyone is in Christ, he is a New Creation, the old has passed away and the new has come." (2 Cor. 5:17) With this new spiritual consciousness we are able to use our Temple for the conscious expression of His Attributes (Divine Wisdom, Love, and Creative Energies) in creation. Dying and being resurrected in the outer world, in the macrocosm, Jesus showed us what will also happen to us, overcoming death the fear of which afflicts all beings who function solely at the level of the personality.

When we partake of the Body and Blood of Christ, Divine Light and Fire come down into ourselves, and this can be a conscious process, a flowing from the Head to the Heart Centers, from above to below. But, as the Light and the Fire come down, so as to bring our consciousness up, they die unto their own level to make us come alive. Thus, Christ historically died for us, but in the continuity of His death and resurrection continues to die with respect to His own level of Consciousness, so as to make us come spiritually alive. When He has thereby raised us and we can draw nearer to Him, and be with him resurrected, then what awaits us is the stage of the Second Coming, His coming in glory, within us and without. In this process, dualism and formal logic become stumbling blocks: between heaven and earth, the separation of body and soul, the sharp contrasts between this life and the next. We not only recognize the linear thread that runs from creation to redemption, and finally to consummation, but also see these fully present as past, present, and future transcendental realities. In the words of Karl Rahner, our "knowledge of the future . . . is an inner moment of the self-understanding of man in his present hour of existence—and grows out of it."[6]

In the last passage, we reaffirm that it is through the Cross of Light and through the Resurrection of Christ, the archetypal and prototypical resurrection of our own spiritual Self, that we are made free to know, to be, and to express our Self; that we are "saved"; and that as Jesus accomplished His mission on earth, so can *we* accomplish it as well. It is truly the Divine Spark, the Inner Christ, who is the Savior of the world, of our very own inner Kingdom as well as of the outer world, and who is the Source and Essence not only of all Life, Love, and Wisdom, but also of *joy*, which is our destiny.

Concluding part of the Eucharistic Prayer

> Priest: "Father, we celebrate the memory of Christ, Your Son. We, Your people and Your ministers, recall His Passion, His Resurrection from the dead, and His ascension into glory; and from the many gifts You have given us we offer to You, God of glory and majesty, the holy and perfect sacrifice: The Bread of Life and the Cup of eternal Salvation."

In this passage, both the Priest and the worshiper "celebrate and recall" (that is, bring back into their consciousness, behold, visualize, contemplate, meditate upon, and recreate within themselves) the Passion of Jesus, His Resurrection from the dead, His Ascension into glory; and the many Gifts He has brought us. This is another way to unite ourselves with the One Whose Being, Deeds, and Life we invoke and seek to relive within ourselves. Specifically, three Deeds and Events of the life of Jesus Christ are evoked and beheld: His Passion, or suffering, His Resurrection from the dead, His Ascension which we are to experience and live in our own being to the degree to which we are, by grace and effort, able.

Finally, it is not the human self, or conscious ego, who can really pray and offer the Living God a worthy sacrifice, but the Divine Spark within us who can offer His own Light and Fire, which engender spiritual Life. Thus, the perfect sacrifice is, indeed, the spiritual Energies, of the Divine Light and Fire.

> "Look with favor on these offerings and accept them as you once accepted the gifts of Your servant Abel, the sacrifices of Abraham, our father in faith, and the bread and wine offered by Your Priest Melchisedech."

Here, a mental evocation and psychospiritual connection is made with a long line of Saints and Sages, spiritual Initiates, of whom Abel, Abraham, and Melchisedech are the prototypes and archetypes, together with their essential deeds. In so doing, the energies, vibrations, and realizations of this long line of Servants of God are reintegrated in the present process, thus reestablishing the Great Chain of Being as well as the interconnections between various levels of the Mystical Body of Christ.

"Almighty God, we pray that Your Angel may take this sacrifice to Your Altar in Heaven, then, as we receive from this Altar the sacred Body and Blood of Your Son, let us be filled with every grace and blessing. Through Christ our Lord. Amen."

The work of the Heavenly Hierarchies, or various Orders of Angels, are clearly mentioned here, recognizing that the Priest at the Altar of the Church (and the conscious ego in the Heart Center) are but the "links" in a long chain of Energy and Light "Transformers." From the sacred traditions, we know that there are Nine Celestial Hierarchies: Angels, Archangels, Principalities, Virtues, Powers, Dominations, Thrones, Cherubim, and Seraphim; the priest and human beings represent the 10th Hierarchy, the final "link" in this long "chain" that connects Heaven and Earth. It is on the Heavenly Altar that the Light and Fire of Christ originate and from which they flow down to the earthly altar of the Church and into the Human Heart Center. Also in sacred tradition, there is an angel who presides at the divine mysteries who presents to God the prayers of the priest and of the people.

"Remember, Lord, those who have died and those who have gone before us marked with the sign of faith, especially those for whom we now pray, N. and M. May these, and all who sleep in Christ, find in Your Presence Light, happiness, and peace. Through Christ our Lord. Amen."

Having opened the channels of Light, Fire, and Life on the vertical dimension from the spiritual world, we now seek to extend these to the whole human family, both to those who are dead and those who are still incarnated on earth and who are not yet spiritually illuminated. This shows that true spiritual Work and Communion with the higher Energies is not an individual but a collective endeavor, and that the essential end of these is to find harmony, healing, enlightenment, and *joy* through the united will, power, and cooperation of the human with the spiritual Self.

"For ourselves, too, we ask some share in the fellowship of your apostles and martyrs, with John the Baptist, Stephen, and all the Saints. Though we are sinners, we trust in Your mercy and love. Do not consider what we truly deserve, but grant us Your forgiveness. Through Christ, our Lord, You give us all these gifts. You fill them with Life and Goodness, You bless them and make them Holy."

Again, an invocation and remembrance of the Saints and Martyrs are made at this point to link ourselves, mentally and telepathically, with them. Martyrs are given the grace of the "short and narrow road" to the top of the Holy Mountain of God. Invoking and beholding this august fellowship can inspire us to persevere in our own spiritual work. There is also the recognition that we are all imperfect and that, even if we do our very best from a human standpoint, we will fall short of perfection and are thus in need of mercy, forgiveness, and love, which we are to also extend to others. This opens up our consciousness and mental and emotional state of mind, makes us more tolerant, flexible, and permeable to the Light and the higher Energies. Finally, we ask that through the Divine Spark within, the bread and wine before us, the vehicles of the Divine Light and Fire, should be blessed and made holy, and activated on the physical plane.

Another version of the concluding part of the Eucharistic Prayer is the following:

> "In memory of His Death and Resurrection, we offer You, Father, this life-giving Bread, this saving Cup. We thank You for counting us worthy to stand in Your Presence and serve You. May all of us who share in the Body and Blood of Christ be brought together in unity by the Holy Spirit.
>
> Lord, remember Your Church throughout the world; make us grow in love, together with our Pope, N., our Bishop M., and all the clergy. Remember N., whom You have called form this life. In Baptism he (she) died with Christ may he (she) also share in His Resurrection.
>
> Remember our brothers and sisters who have gone to their rest in the hope of rising again; bring them and all the departed into the Light of Your Presence. Have mercy on us all; make us worthy to share eternal Life with Mary, the Virgin Mother of God, with the Apostles, and with all the Saints who have done Your Will throughout the ages. May we praise You in union with them, and give Your Glory through Your Son, Jesus Christ."

A final version of the concluding part of the Eucharistic Prayer, which fulfills the same purpose as the previous ones, is the following:

> "Father, we now celebrate this memorial of redemption. We recall Christ's Death, His descent among the dead, His Resurrection, and His Ascension to Your right hand; and, looking forward to His coming in

Glory, we offer You His Body and Blood, the acceptable sacrifice which brings salvation to the whole world.

Lord, look upon this sacrifice which You have given Your Church; and by Your Holy Spirit, gather all who share this Bread and Wine into the One Body of Christ, a living sacrifice of praise.

Lord, remember those for whom we offer this sacrifice, especially N. our Pope, M. our Bishop, and the clergy everywhere. Remember those who have died in the peace of Christ and all the dead whose faith is known to You alone. Father, in Your mercy grant also to us, your children, to enter into our heavenly inheritance in the company of the Virgin Mary, the Mother of God, and Your Apostles and Saints. Then, in Your Kingdom, freed from the corruption of sin and death, we shall sing Your Glory with every creature through Christ our Lord, through Whom You give us everything that is good."

Though the versions of the Eucharistic Prayer are different, their essential function is the same: to establish in our consciousness, and through us in the world, the Communion of Saints, the great Mystical Body of Christ, the Great Chain of Being, wherein we are all consciously connected and related to all beings and all parts of creation, both within ourselves and in the world, offering praise and thanksgiving to God. It is the celebration of all the gifts He gives us, of our being worthy to stand in His presence and serve Him. Within us, Christ is present as our Divine Spark, the spiritual Self, in the microcosm of our human nature; so, too, the Virgin Mary is present as the Soul, that which mediates between the self and the Self within human consciousness, in the microcosm. They work within us and with us, along with the hierarchy of angels, the saints, martyrs, the prophets of old, the more so as we consciously align ourselves within with them, in helping us to be more who we are, actualize our potentials, leading us to attain spiritual illumination and salvation, and realize our destiny in union with God and with each other. And this is what is represented by, and underlies, the concept and experience of the "Mystical Body of Christ" and of the "Communion of Saints:" *the overcoming, from the spiritual and the human side, of separation, which brings about loneliness and selfishness, and the restoration of the continuity of Consciousness and Life amongst all beings and parts of creation, in heaven and on earth.*

Doxology

> "Through Him, with Him, in Him, in the unity of the Holy Spirit, all glory and honor is Yours, Almighty Father, for ever and ever. Amen. Amen. Amen."

This passage, in its spiritual meaning, summarizes the Eucharistic Prayer by affirming the progression and bringing to consciousness of what we are now to experience, the Holy Trinity is vibrantly present here and can be consciously related across the threefold nature of our being, as the genius of each individual can experience that in their Will, Heart, and Head centers. That this process serves to glorify and honor the Almighty Father throughout all eternity, as it is now and forever present, completes the exchange, which is sealed with the "Amen," the "so be it" according to Thy will—and this, too, is realized across our threefold nature.

The Communion Rite

Here, all stand while the Lord's Prayer is recited or sung by all. The priest prefaces this in saying: "Let us now pray in the words our Savior gave to us." This recalls for us the fact that this is the prayer of Jesus Christ to His and our Heavenly Father, thus revealing to us the deepest essence of how we are to pray. Internally it acts as a "spiritual elixir," activating our entire being and consciousness, resonating in each of our psychospiritual Centers of awareness, cleansing and consecrating our Energy Bodies, awakening our spiritual faculties, all so we may be able to commune with Our Lord, both as He is within us and without, in heaven and on earth. It is, therefore, the perfect and complete prayer, which is always used theurgically in order to achieve union. It is the final touch before actually going to Communion.[7]

> Priest: "Deliver us, Lord, from every evil, and grant us peace in our day. In Your mercy keep us free from sin and protect us from all anxiety as we wait in joyful hope for the coming of our Savior, Jesus Christ."

These lines reiterate the last line of the Lord's Prayer, as they reiterate the fact that once we are opened and consecrated, as has been the process of the Mass accomplished to here, we are still not free from temptation. With God's mercy we are able to recognize evil for what it is and not be overcome or overwhelmed by it. From an esoteric viewpoint, what most harms human beings is their own evil or sins, because they cut them off from God and from who they truly are. To spiritual consciousness, nothing truly evil or harmful can happen. Finally, in preserving our peace is a sense of maintaining our connectedness or harmony with the Whole. It is in sin and lack of peace, separation or break from the Whole, that true anxiety originates. Thus, delivered from evil, sin, and anxiety, we wait in joyful hope for the coming in Glory of our Savior, both as the Christ within us and as He is manifest in history.

Doxology

> People: "For the Kingdom, the Power, and the Glory are Yours, now and forever."

From a spiritual viewpoint, this is an integral part of the Lord's Prayer and should be linked and interpreted with it. It is the Christian version of the Qabalistic Cross that seals our energy bodies and fixes in our consciousness and psychospiritual centers the work that has been done.

The Sign of Peace

> Priest: "Lord Jesus Christ, You said to Your Apostles: I leave you peace, My peace I give unto you. Look not on our sins, but on the faith of Your Church, and grant us the Peace and Unity of Your Kingdom where You live for ever and ever."
> People: "Amen."
> Priest: "The Peace of the Lord be with you always."
> People: "And also with you."
> Priest: "Let us offer each other the sign of peace."

Peace is this inner and outer harmony, connection and deep relationship, which establishes and permeates the Communion of Saints; it bonds heaven and earth, and unites God and Man. Thus, it is a basic quality of true spiritual enlightenment; together with the Gift of the Holy Spirit (the vivifying Life of our whole being and consciousness), the peace of God is what is bequeathed to us by Jesus Christ's own Spirit, so that we may make that peace visible in our lives. Thus, at this point, just before the actual Communion takes place, Light is extended from the Altar to the people, from the Heart Center to our whole being, and from the Priest to the worshipers, as well as from the worshipers to each other. Here, there is an actual circulation of Light and Energy as contact is made on various levels among the worshipers, as they touch each other and as they extend a sign of peace to each other. In this circulation, this Light and Energy flows from the spiritual to the physical and from the physical back to the spiritual level, within and among the worshipers.

The Breaking of the Bread

> "Lamb of God, You take away the sins of the world: have mercy on us.
> Lamb of God, You take away the sins of the world: have mercy on us.
> Lamb of God, You take away the sins of the world: grant us peace."

The "Lamb of God" is, of course, Jesus Christ, in the total surrender of His being to the Will of God; He is the Sacrificial Lamb, without blemish, who offers Himself to God in atonement for the sins of the world. In the purity and ardor of this divine act we can experience here the Lamb as Divine Light and Divine Fire, perfectly attuned and obedient to the Will of God. This Light and Fire, descending from above, we experience primarily in the three highest Centers, flowing down throughout our being, especially from the Left Shoulder Center (since the esoteric virtue here is mercy), throughout our entire Tree of Life.

Communion

> Priest: "This is the Lamb of God Who takes away the sins of the world. Happy are those who are called to His supper."
> All: "Lord, I am not worthy to receive You but only say the Word and I shall be healed."

This is the true culmination of the Mass; as we move up to the Altar, we move as well to our heart of hearts, to receive the Body and Blood of Our Lord. To receive the Divine Light and Divine Fire, which none can merit save but by what He Himself can remedy in our deficiencies, we can approach with fervent desire, for it is here that the fervor, the dedication, and the concentration of the faithful should reach its maximum degree. Here, the bread and wine, while retaining their external appearance of bread and wine, through the action of the Holy Spirit working through the agency of the Angelic Hierarchies and of the Priest, have become the instruments or vehicles for the Body and Blood of Christ—the Divine Light and the Divine Fire, which engender Life on all levels and planes of being. Like the wires that carry the electrical current in its positive and negative polarities once the current is turned on, so the Bread and Wine become the channels and physical vehicles for the Divine Light and Fire of the Christ. Hence they are, indeed, objectively and empirically, the "Lamb of God Who takes away the sins of the world". The paradox here is that no human being is really worthy to receive the Body and Blood of Christ, and yet it is precisely for sinners, imperfect people, that this rite has been instituted. Thus, the more we have fallen short of our ideals and given way to negative thoughts, feelings, impulses, words, and deeds, *the more we need to commune with the Divine Light and Fire!*

Each will welcome Him into their being in their own individual way. Here is how I personally prepare myself for this magnificent experience: In raising my consciousness my attention, my thoughts and particularly my feelings, from my Shoulder Centers and my Heart Center to my Head Center, I say three times: "O Lord Jesus Christ, Son of God, Savior, have mercy upon me a sinner." Then, continuing:

> For I acknowledge and I confess that Thou are the Christ, the Son of the Living God, and that this is, in very truth, Thine immaculate Body and this Thy precious Blood. Grant that, though infinitely unworthy, I may partake of thine all holy, all healing, and life-giving Mysteries. That they may come for the healing of my Soul and of my body, for the remission of my sins and transgressions, that I may lead a more holy, constructive, and creative life, and that I may inherit Life-eternal.

When going to Communion, it is left to each to experience the difference in taking the Eucharist from the celebrating priest and directly into one's mouth rather than in one's hand, submitting that to obtain the maximum effects at the conscious level, it is better that the Divine Light and Fire, which engender the spiritual Life, enter the Energy Bodies and the psychospiritual Centers of the worshipers through their mouths.

After Communion, one returns to kneel or sit in prayer or meditate in thanksgiving. St. Alphonsus de Liguori advises us to spend at least a short time in conversing with Jesus Christ:

> the soul, than that which is made during the thanksgiving after Communion . . . St. Teresa of Avila says, that after Communion Christ places himself in the soul as on a throne of grace, and then says: what willest thou that I should do for thee? (Mark 5:51) meaning, O soul, I am come for the express purpose of granting thee graces: ask me what thou wilt, and as much as thou willest, thou shalt receive all.

Having received Communion, I go back to my seat and, seated, inwardly go through the following meditation, repeating the above prayer of mine but now consciously extending it throughout my being and consciousness:

> For I acknowledge and I confess that Thou art the Christ, the Son of the living God, and that This is Your precious Body and that This is your precious Blood. Though infinitely unworthy, grant that I may receive Them so that Thou wouldst fill my spiritual body (and I focus my attention upon my spiritual body), my mental body (and I direct my attention to my mental body), my emotional body (and I direct my attention to my emotional body), and my vital and physical body (and I direct my attention to my vital/physical body), with Thy Divine Light, Fire, and Life. and I conclude: Fill Thou also my Head Center

> (and I direct my consciousness to my Head Center, attempting to visualize and to feel the Divine Light, Fire, and Life entering that Center and activating it), my Left Cheek Center (same as before), my Right Cheek Center (same as before), my Left Shoulder Center (same as before), my Right Shoulder Center (same as before), my Heart Center (same as before), my Left Hip Center (same as before), my Right Hip Center (same as before), my Sexual Center (same as before), and my Feet Center (same as before), with Thy Divine Light, Fire, and Life.

Then, as the Light and Fire descend into and fill my whole Tree of Life and all of its Centers, vivifying them, I remain a few moments in silence to fully absorb what is happening. I finish with one fervent exhortation into which I pour my whole consciousness, heart, mind, soul, and spirit:

> O Lord, heal me, make me whole, enable me to know Thee as my One true God, and to attune my consciousness with Thine, so that I may use all of my time, energies, faculties, opportunities, and resources in the most constructive and useful way—so that I may fulfill my work and destiny on earth.

Concluding Rite

Priest: "The Lord be with you."
People: "And also with you."
Priest: "May almighty God bless, you, the Father, the Son, and the Holy Spirit."

People: "Amen."
Priest:
A. "Go in the peace of Christ."
B. "The Mass is ended, go in peace."
C. "Go in peace to love and serve the Lord."
People: "Thanks be to God."

In the Eucharist, one finds the very Source and Essence of all Life, Love, and Wisdom and the way to a living connection with them. One finds and fulfills the deep longing of heart and soul; one aspires but is inspired; one reaches out but is reached out to.

Here quests end and quests begin: one finds the Holy Grail, the cup of our salvation overflowing with bliss, the radiant splendor of God's Love; the wisdom of ages sought in the Philosopher's stone as key to true, integral knowledge of oneself, Man, God, and Nature, the keys to His Kingdom; the *Elixir Vitae,* the draught of eternal life; the panacea, the medicine to heal all ills. What can you seek that is not found here? At the end of our seeking, He is there; but now uniting Himself with us, a new life begins and His seeking is ours. He wills through us a more perfect love, a love conformable to His Perfect Love for all creation. How this Love and Light will break across the spectrum of each individual consciousness is alone for each to experience uniquely as oneself reunited with God. Only silence speaks further of this great Mystery; but what has spoken if not this silence in all heroic deeds?

The final blessing concludes and seals the whole movement so as to retain the Inner Light and Fire, with their concomitant level of consciousness, for as long as possible. And this blessing is now given in a very different state of conscious awareness than before; it now remains to go and love, to go and serve, in full consciousness, Jesus Christ.

The Mass is an inexhaustible treasure which can be experienced many times, each time in an absolutely fresh and unique way never known before and never, perhaps, to be known again in quite the same way. When each ritual comes alive, when the Mass is lived consciously, there is a quality of freshness, of uniqueness, and of spontaneous discovery, which is like entering a glorious garden, indescribably fragrant, ripe with fruits, bright with flowers, alive with docile beasts and singing birds: an organic image for an organic process—and a cumulative one. The more one goes to Mass and Communion, and especially, the more one brings oneself there in consciousness, mind, heart, and will, gathering meanings and purposes and entering into the fullness of devotion, the more one begins to recognize this garden, this infinitely beautiful and eternal garden, as what He prepares within us, a place worthy of Himself, a place where He can speak to us, teach us, and unfold for us His wondrous mysteries. And unfold *us,* for it can literally seem that we are only now beginning to arise from the dead, to *wake up* and discover what we and life are all about. Then, all that is left to do is truly to *live one's life as a work of art, fulfilling God's will and destiny, as the sacred dance of life, love, light, and joy*. And since that is the domain of silence and of personally lived experience, this is the point where this chapter ends—and where *your* experience should begin.

CHAPTER TWO

Levels on the Vertical Axis of Human Consciousness

It is very easy to see—in fact it happens every day—that exactly the same situation, event, or external condition can be experienced and lived in very different ways by different persons, or even by the same person at different times or in different states of consciousness. Obviously, all depends on how this person perceives, conceives, defines, and reacts—at the spiritual, mental, emotional, and physical level—to a given existential situation. And this, in turn, depends on his or her level of consciousness and being.

What this means, in other words, is that our way of perceiving, conceiving, and reacting to reality or to a specific situation is a function of our level of consciousness and being. When we change our level of consciousness, we concomitantly change our perception, conception, and reaction to reality. This notion was well known by the ancients and by the sacred traditions. This is why the quintessence of Greek Wisdom was expressed in the famous "Man, know thyself!" which was inscribed on Greek Temples. We find the same insight in the concept of the "magical mirror," of the "sphere of sensation" in the magical, hermetic, and alchemical traditions. In the words of Evelyn Underhill, referring to the higher levels of consciousness:

> It is indeed only when he reaches these levels, and feels within himself this creative freedom—the full actualization of himself—on the one hand; on the other hand the sense of a world-order, a love and energy on which he depends and with whose interests he is now at one, that man becomes fully human, capable of living the real life of Eternity in the midst of the world of time.[1]

This insight, and the concept which embodies it, are essential to properly understand the reactions of people located on different levels of what I call the "vertical axis of consciousness."

The core point of this basic insight, which I represent today with the image of Man, the skyscraper, is the following:

Each human being can be represented by a skyscraper with one hundred floors. That is, there exists within us an axis of qualitatively different levels of consciousness. There also exists an "elevator", a means of making the human self and its field of consciousness go up and down this axis, as an elevator would climb to the one hundredth floor or go down to the first floor. Herein lies the true key, or substance of human growth and spiritual awakening and of true progress, which consists in knowing this "elevator" and how it goes up and down, how it rises to a superior level.

Let us now explore it a little further with this analogy.

If we enter a skyscraper and look outside from the first, tenth, fortieth, eightieth, or one hundredth floor, what we "see," our perception of reality, changes dramatically. Below, we have "myopic" vision and perception, limited to what is immediately in front of the skyscraper at this level. But the higher we rise, the more our vision, our physical perceptions, changes, such that reality is apprehended as a whole with a vision that is far greater and more complete. The same thing happens when we climb to the top of a mountain or when we climb in an airplane. To rise means to see and thus to understand wholes that are greater and greater. To descend means diminished sight, or to see only parts or fragments that become smaller and smaller.

What we see when we look out of the window on the first, twentieth, or one hundredth floor is just as real and true but it is not the same view. A proper grasp of this can greatly help us to understand and thus to accept people who function on different levels of consciousness and being, that is to say, who are located on "different floors," and to do this without getting angry at them, blaming them, or seeking to convert them to our perceptions, conceptions, and values. To use another analogy, we all go through the various stages, or ages of the human lifecycle: the infant, the child, the adolescent, and the adult. What we expect of an adult is certainly not what we expect of a baby. Moreover, there is an organic growth that leads the baby to slowly become the adult. This process is at first unconscious, that is, does not depend on our will or on our conscious cooperation; but it becomes more and more conscious, depending on our willing cooperation and commitment.

Our level of consciousness and being plays an absolutely vital role for all that we consider most real and important—for our sense of identity, our perceptions, conceptions, and reactions to external reality, as well as for the expression of the seven functions of our psyche: in particular, for willing, thinking, and feeling. Hence, it also plays an essential role in our relationships to religion, politics, economics, morality, love, and health.

To better illustrate and render more concrete this fundamental insight and image, I would like to tell a story. Imagine a famous professor, holding several degrees and of international repute. He is working in his studio, located on the first floor of his house. His son is playing in the garden where there are trees. They are waiting for the professor's brother, who is coming with his wife and their three children on the 3:40 P.M. train. It takes about twenty minutes to go by foot from the house of the professor to the train station.

At 3:20 P.M., the son of the professor climbs on a tree about thirty feet from the ground. Looking around him, the professor's son sees, on the road that leads to the house, two adults and two children who are approaching the house. Very happy, he yells: "Daddy, Daddy, there they are, they are coming—my uncle, my aunt, and my cousins." The professor looks at his watch, shakes his head, and answers: "Come on, it is only 3:22 P.M.; it is impossible, their train has not even arrived yet. They must be other people." But a few minutes later, the two adults and their children arrive, and indeed, it is the uncle, the aunt, and the nephews. They had simply taken the previous train, which arrived at 3:00 P.M.!

The reasoning of the illustrious professor was perfectly correct, in relation to what he knew. But as he was located on a lower level than his son who had climbed on a tree, in spite of all his knowledge and intelligence, he could not see what his son could see directly. He perceived reality in a different fashion.

This is the essential point: there exists a simultaneous growth and development of the faculties of human consciousness on the horizontal and on the vertical levels: on the vertical level in quality, going from one level to another; and on the horizontal level in quantity or degree, but remaining on the same qualitative level. This can explain many paradoxes, antinomies, and contradictions, as well as the extraordinary diversity of viewpoints that human beings have. There are, in fact, human beings endowed with a great intelligence and sensibility who perceive, conceive, and define reality in a certain way (which is underpinned by their present level of consciousness), and who react to given situations in conformity with their level of consciousness. We could cite, for example, Freud, Marx, and Voltaire. But, there are also other human beings, equally bright and sensitive, such as Plato, Bergson, and Assagioli, who perceive and define reality in opposite ways and who react very differently to the same specific situation. This is historical and academic fact.

For me, it is clearly the notion of the vertical and qualitative axis of consciousness of a person that can help explain the great diversity and complexity of conceptions of reality, of ethical values, and of religious and political conceptions of human beings. Hence, it is this fundamental intuition that can help us to reconcile opposites such as Matter-Spirit (materialism-spiritualism), egoism-altruism, pessimism-optimism, or hope-despair. It can also help make sense of the "vertical" psychiatric paradox of people who fall sick or have a nervous breakdown or who "burn out" because of very ordinary pressures and disappointments, while others remain healthy and psychologically integrated even in worse situations and under extreme pressures and sufferings. Finally, it is also here that we can begin to understand how the same religion can be interpreted and lived in one way by some people and in a different, if not opposite way, by others; that prayer accomplishes nothing for some while it can literally work miracles for others; and that going to Communion can be a very normal and unconscious experience for some, while it is the most intense, profound, and life-giving experience for others. And this would also help explain why, with the passage of time, with human growth and the expansion of human consciousness, things do change and transform themselves, both inwardly, or subjectively, and outwardly, or objectively.

In the material world, we find a phenomenon that is very rare in creation and that affords a unique opportunity for personal growth: namely, the fact that human beings, souls, of very different levels of consciousness and being meet, become aware of each other, and interact. This situation greatly facilitates and stimulates the growth, the opening of consciousness, and the self-actualization of all those who are thus involved. The sacred traditions have taught us for a long time that in the inner psychic and spiritual world, only beings who are on the same "wavelength" and who find themselves on the same level of consciousness and being, meet, become aware of each other, and can interact in a meaningful and real way. This, by the way, has now been fully corroborated by people who have had NDEs and OBEs (near-death experiences and out-of-the-body experiences).

What this means, practically speaking, is that a person who raises or lowers their level of consciousness and being will see others disappear to their vision and no longer be there. This is precisely what occurs at the death of a person, when the physical body is destroyed and when the human self and its field of consciousness move from the physical body to the soul.

In the invisible worlds, on the psychic and spiritual planes (etheric, astral, mental, and spiritual) there is a force that acts as gravitation does on the physical plane, in such a way that people find themselves, "see," and interact on the same "wavelength" and on the same "plane." Thus, those who are above or below a certain "wavelength," who are on different planes, whether higher or lower, do not see and cannot meet or interact with each other. There exists a true separation, just as television programs on different frequencies are separated. This law, however, does not hold for the physical world, or the earthly material plane. Here, we all have the great challenge and the marvelous growth opportunity to meet and interact with beings who are on higher or lower floors than ours.

This is also the reason why Love, which transforms multiplicity into unity and which establishes right relationships between parts and wholes, is the only force in the universe that can reunite and reconcile opposites, connect the strong and the weak, the rich and the poor, the high and the low. Love is the force and energy that binds all worlds and dimensions, all levels of consciousness and being, especially in the material world, which presents such huge differences and varieties of beings.

It is also interesting to note how, in the material world, union and fusion generate and free up energy, while separation consumes energy. On the human level, union brings joy, happiness, peace, and health, just as on the spiritual plane union brings growth, harmony, and Life, opening the gates of Paradise—of our Communion and Reunion with God—while separation brings devolution, anxiety, death, and opens the doors of Hell.

This brings us to the heart of our discussion on the image and analogy of Man the skyscraper. At the center of the skyscraper we find an "elevator" with "buttons" that can make it go up or down. The elevator represents the human self with the field of consciousness and its seven functions and muscles. It is precisely these muscles of human consciousness (representing the "buttons") that, when properly applied, make the elevator go up or down. The skyscraper itself represents the vertical and qualitative axis of our consciousness. To each level of being and loving corresponds a certain level, frequency or state of our consciousness, and vice versa.

This is why when we change our level of being and loving we also change automatically our level of consciousness. When we change our level or frequency of consciousness, our level of being and loving rises or falls. It is also here that *purification, consecration,* and *communion* with the spiritual Self comes into play as a major way of expanding our consciousnesses, and thus growing and raising our level of being and our capacity to love.

Fasting and praying, emptying and filling our being, are ways in which we can effect movement between levels of consciousness and being. Yet maybe the simplest, most direct, and most effective way to make the elevator rise to the higher floors is the proper use of *Faith,* which we can experience in opening our heart, mind, and soul and directing all of our attention, thoughts, and feelings on a chosen point on top of the skyscraper.

If we carry through with this analogy, the one hundred floors of the skyscraper represent, symbolically: the unconscious and what is also called "Hell" (the basements and the first five floors); the subconscious and what is also called "Purgatory" (the fifth to the twentieth floor); the preconscious and the field of consciousness, called the "Earth" (the twentieth to the fortieth floor); finally, the Superconscious, also called "Heaven" (the fortieth to the one hundredth floor). Thus, in learning how to make the elevator go up and down, we need the keys of Heaven and Hell, which we could call today the opening of the Superconscious and of the unconscious.

The central point of our discussion of the vertical axis of consciousness and being is the following: What does it mean and what are the implications of going "up and down" this axis? The expansion and transformation of human consciousness can take place on two axes that must, ultimately, be integrated. On the vertical axis, it can go up or down and on the horizontal axis, it can expand out or unfold. Our modern scientific culture emphasizes quantity rather than quality, analysis rather than synthesis, and has focused its explorations and analyses almost exclusively on the horizontal axis, on having more or less, rather than on being and on qualitative growth.

Our educational system, our society, and our literature (with the exception of the sacred, spiritual, and religious traditions) lead us with incredible force, either consciously or unconsciously, to seek and possess only quantity, to have more or less of this or of that. Today, we are witnessing an incredible paradox whereby people have always more and are always less happy. Maybe this is what Jesus foresaw when He stated: "What does it benefit a man if he gains the whole world but loses his soul?" Or what Max Weber predicted when he told us that the "disenchantment of the world" would come; or what Ralph W. Emerson intuited in his fundamental question: "Modern civilization has built enormous buildings and built powerful machines, but what has it done for the human beings who live in these buildings and who drive these machines?"

Today, it is imperative that we make the transition from having to being, from quantity to quality. We must rediscover the vertical axis of consciousness and being and learn how to move consciously on this axis. How to go up or down on this axis is a vital question. It is literally vital because above we find Life, Consciousness, Love, Liberty, Joy, the Self and Being while below we have death, unconsciousness, Indifference, Hatred, Slavery, Suffering, and Alienation—nonbeing.

Moreover, going up or down has a direct and vital impact on the three "royal faculties" of the psyche, as well as upon a number of other functions. It determines thinking, feeling, and willing; that is, consciousness, knowledge, love, and self-expression or creativity. Moving up we understand what was before incomprehensible, we discover new meanings, and thinking becomes clear and precise; while moving down we go towards noncomprehension, the lack of meaning. Going up, we become able to love, to feel deeply and passionately, we discover the taste of life, the world and human experience; while going down we move towards indifference, disgust, and frustration, and we lose the joy of living. Going up, we succeed in being ourselves and expressing our selves, we change our personality and the world to create, to make a difference; while going down, we fall into alienation, we become strangers to our Self, to life, and to the world.

When we move up, the images, the symbols, the myths, and the rituals of the sacred traditions speak to us and unveil their Mysteries, their deeper implications and applications; while when we go down they cease to speak, they veil their Mysteries and become superstitions and illusions. Going up, human beings become capable of accepting all the parts and aspects of themselves, of the world and of life, and of integrating and reconciling them; while going down they accept certain aspects and reject others, thus entering into conflict with one's self and with the world. Going up, one discovers Being, God, and therefore Faith, Hope, and Charity, while going down, one discovers the Devil, hence, separation, doubt, despair, and egoism.

It is only in moving up that one discovers peace, serenity, and both inner and outer harmony, while it is in going down that one falls into conflict, disharmony, and both inner and outer strife, and therefore, that one becomes ill. It is above that one finds unity, the holistic or global vision of reality, while below we find multiplicity and a myopic and partial vision of reality. It is truly above, in the Superconscious and in the Self, that one can find the Source and Essence of Life, of Love, and of Knowledge that must vivify matter. Above we have the reconciliation of opposites, union, and true synthesis, while below we fall, inevitably, into paradoxes, antinomies, separation, and conflicts. This is why Roberto Assagioli used to say that: "Below, there are no real solutions to the most important human problems, while 'above' there are no problems." One of the basic injunctions of the Primordial Tradition has always been to "Seek first the Kingdom of God and His Justice"; that is, to rise to the higher levels of consciousness to awaken spiritual consciousness so that "all these things shall be given unto you": the true solution to all our problems, the right measure and proportion for all things, and the awakening of our intuition.

On the physical plane, things work pretty much the same way: our perception, conception, and definition of reality change radically as we climb the Holy Mountain. What we can see, hear, smell, taste, and touch on the first floor, on the tenth, fortieth, or hundredth is absolutely not the same thing, just as when we climb a mountain, reality changes dramatically as we move from three hundred feet to one thousand feet, and then to three thousand feet. From above, we have a global view where parts blend to form a comprehensible whole. While from below we have a partial view of the parts which, alone and unconnected, has no meaning, integration, or purpose. The perception of a given place is radically different for the butterfly than it is for the caterpillar. Also, as we climb higher, learning how to fly like the birds, to rise above negative situations, we can avoid a great many dangers, illnesses, and conflicts.

Finally, one finds the same principle and the same lesson at work in human societies, for instance in social stratification. The more we rise on the social and professional scale, the more reality and the experiences we live change. Above one is unique and irreplaceable, while below one is very replaceable—today even by a machine. The sociocultural experience of a taxi driver in a one-star hotel or in a diner is dramatically different from that of a prime minister in a five-star hotel or in a very expensive restaurant. One can even find, in the same society, the paradox and apparent injustice that below there are people who are dying of hunger, while above there are people who can eat all they want—delicious meals in the best restaurants that might even be too much for their health.

One can say that life, love, creativity, understanding, peace, justice, freedom, self-expression, health, happiness, and *joie de vivre* can only be found above, in the higher states of consciousness, in paradise, and never below in the lower states of consciousness, in Hell. Hence, the fundamental choice, the most important thing in all situations, is always that of knowing how and being able to climb higher towards paradise where the Self and God can be found together with all that one could ever desire or dream of. Likewise, to avoid many dangers, difficult situations, and disasters, one must learn how to fly like the birds, higher always higher! This is, I believe, the key to the art of living in our times when we are discovering the keys of Heaven and Hell, the opening of the unconscious and the superconscious.

It is also here that one can begin to find authentic solutions to the great human problems: the problems of religion, science, philosophy, as well as those of morality, politics, economics, medicine, and education. In the ultimate analysis, everything is a function of our level of consciousness and of our level of being. This is the reason that in human life we find so many paradoxes, contradictions, seeming injustices, and no real and effective "solutions," but only a long journey inside of ourselves towards the top of the Holy Mountain where the Self, the Divine Spark, and the living Christ await us.

One of the great gifts of Heaven and certainly the most important treasure I have found in this world, has been to meet and to interact with a very wide variety of human beings who cover most of the human spectrum. Thus, I have met ordinary people of various countries and cultures, as well as criminals, idiots, and insane people at the "bottom" of the scale, and geniuses, saints, and spiritually awakened persons at the "top" of the scale. One thing that struck me in these encounters, which I have noted several times in my diary, was the enormous diversity of their perceptions, conceptions, and definitions of reality, of the world, of human beings, and of the various human problems. I was so impressed that

I wrote a book (*Spiritual Man in the Modern World*), to try to explain and make sense of this incredible diversity. Even though we are all living on the same earth and world of matter, it is now clear to me that there are people who come from and live in worlds that are very, very different, and who have a very different system of values, priorities, desires, and points of reference. It is this realization that made me finally understand the famous Platonic analogy that there are human beings who have "gold," "silver," "bronze," and "iron" in their "hearts." That is, there are people whose basic values and most important desires are quite different, if not incompatible. Some seek knowledge and the love of God above all (those who have "gold" in their "hearts"); some seek power (those who have "silver" in their "hearts"); and others seek security (those who have "bronze" in their "hearts") or pleasures (those who have "iron" in their "hearts"). It is the insight and the image of "Man the skyscraper" that helped me to understand, rationally, these differences, as well as to understand the paradoxes, antinomies, contradictions, and conflicts that more and more confront the citizens of our "global village." This is absolutely essential for a true understanding of human beings who find themselves on different levels of consciousness and being.

Another basic principle concerning this insight is the following: People who are on higher levels of consciousness and being can always descend and understand those who are on lower levels by making efforts to lower their lights and vibrations, and level of consciousness. On the other hand, those who are on a lower level of consciousness cannot readily rise and understand those who are on higher levels, but may, for a brief moment, be "pulled up," as it were, by the presence and the "radiations" of people who are on "higher levels." To illustrate this, I will tell you the story of a couple of real situations that I have personally lived.

Once I met a boy who was a petty thief who lived and helped his family by what he could take or steal from others. After some time, we developed a friendship and talked a great deal. Often he would ask me, in all confidence, why I never tried to take things from him or from others, and, especially, why I gave things away, made presents, and never expected anything in return. For him, this was totally incomprehensible. One day, he even told me, with an incredible archetypal and symbolic meaning, "It's as though I was an inhabitant of the earth and you of the sun!" I do not tell this story to liken myself to the sun, but to illustrate that the basic, most fundamental, tendency of the earth is to take, while that of the sun is to give and to radiate. The first is, also, the basic tendency of the personality, while the second is the essential tendency of the individuality or of the Soul; whence we have the great contradiction between egoism and altruism, two basic and opposed tendencies that one finds, in different degrees, in all people.

The other story is the following: I met and became friends with a man and a woman who came from very prominent families and who had great wealth. Both were very drawn to and interested in spirituality and spiritual teachings and the esoteric dimension. Moreover, both were at the level of consciousness and being that I call that of the "disciple," of the "great turning point," "metamorphosis," or "conversion." Both had traveled a great deal throughout the world. They had the means, the time, and the social contacts to meet all the people they were most interested in, including clairvoyants, healers, gurus, Nobel Prize winners, and internationally recognized "saints." When we got to know each other better and had reached a certain level of intimacy, both of them asked me: "Do truly spiritually awakened persons with exceptional powers, knowledge, goodness, and creativity really exist? And if so, where are they and how can we meet them? All the people we have met who should have been in that category really were not, and were basically ordinary people with a little more vitality, intelligence, courage, and ambition—or obsession!" These two people who were so cosmopolitan, with so much money, many opportunities, and social contacts were, deep down, disillusioned, sad, and basically skeptical. Why and how can one explain this?

The answer, I believe, is quite simple: they sought in the world that which they first had to discover and activate in themselves. That is, they remained blocked on a certain level and perceived and interpreted everything on this level, even people who could have been authentic and superior, but who remained undecipherable enigmas, and who did not unveil or manifest their superior nature, knowledge, and capacities. We can only truly understand that which is on our level and that which is below, but not that which is above. Once we have really understood the great discovery, or conclusion, of modern physics: that everything, absolutely everything in our universe—that is, the entire reality knowable by human beings—is vibration, energy and light vibrating at different frequencies, then we grasp and understand this great arcana of the sacred traditions: That we can perceive correctly and truly understand only that which is found on our level of human consciousness and being.

Once we accept the new, yet ancient, conception of human nature as being composed of four and not three basic ages, or levels of maturity—the biological, emotional, mental, and spiritual age—then we shall realize and accept, logically and naturally, that there are human beings on different levels of consciousness and being, and that reality is something quite different for them, corresponding to their specific level. And then we shall be able to develop a differential anthropology, psychology, and sociology of each type, with characteristics that are peculiar to their level of perceiving, conceiving, defining, and reacting to the same situation in their own specific ways. Taking as a basic point of reference the three royal functions of the psyche—willing, thinking, and feeling—and the seven chakras of the Eastern Spiritual Traditions, I have attempted to set up a tentative "hierarchy of human beings" on seven different levels of consciousness and being.

In our personality, or "lower self," we find a certain activity and expression of these three functions, as we find them again but transformed at the level of the "individuality," or "higher self." Between the personality and the individuality, we find the psychospiritual center of the Heart. It is truly the opening, activation, and awakening of the Heart Center which constitutes the great passage, Initiation, or transformation from being a slave to the personality and its desires to being free from the compulsions and obsessions of the lower self; and from living in the world of illusions to living in the world of Eternal Reality. Likewise, when we look at the chakras of the Eastern traditions, we discover that the first three chakras govern our instincts and survival impulses at the physical, emotional, and mental levels; while the last three govern the expression of the Divine Wisdom, Love, and Will. And it is at the level of the fourth chakra, or Heart Center, that we find the great passage or transformation from the mortal, human, and egoistical ("geotropic") dimension to the eternal, spiritual, and altruistic ("heliotropic") one.

Starting from the bottom up, I would set up the following tentative hierarchy and set of correspondences:

1. First chakra: human will, instinct, impulses—primitive persons.
2. Second chakra: human emotions, desires, egoism—ordinary persons.
3. Third chakra: human thoughts, egoism—talented persons.
4. Fourth chakra: Heart Center, Love Initiation, passage from the "rule of the personality" to the "rule of the individuality"—true disciples of the authentic spiritual schools and Masters.
5. Fifth chakra: spiritually illuminated thoughts—Geniuses.
6. Sixth chakra: spiritually illuminated emotions—Saints.
7. Seventh chakra: spiritually illuminated will—true Masters.

As all functions of a person's psyche, and in particular, the three "royal forces," are functions at person's levels of consciousness and being, it follows that there are seven types of human beings which constitute the natural hierarchy of the world of matter. Each type will perceive, conceive, define, and react in qualitatively different ways to all human conditions and situations. For instance, this means that we will have seven qualitatively different ways of perceiving, conceiving, defining, and reacting to religion, politics, economics; of understanding and expressing knowledge, love, and will; of perceiving and reacting to illnesses, accidents, injustices, suffering, and the manifold experiences of life on earth. Moreover, we will also have seven qualitatively different hierarchies of values and moral principles. For example, on the level of the first chakra, there is an iron rule whereby everything, without exception, is immediately related to one's body, instincts, desires, and interests; while on the level of the seventh chakra there is also an iron rule whereby everything, without exception, is immediately related to the Self, to God, and to the common good. This is because at the lower levels we perceive and define ourselves as our "physical body," while at the higher levels we perceive and define ourselves as the "Self" which manifests itself through the bodies and the souls of all human beings.

Primitive, ordinary, and talented persons correspond to the "Work of Nature," and to the stages of the "infant," the "child," and the "adolescent," respectively, while Geniuses, Saints, and Masters correspond to the "Work of Art," and to the stages of the "adult, the mature person, and the old person." To reach these levels, human cooperation, conscious evolution, and serious work in which each person practices "personality" and "Soul Sculpture" are necessary, because without the conscious and focused use of our will, thoughts, and feelings, we are unlikely to reach the higher levels. As for the "Disciples," they represent the "Great Passage," the "initiation of the heart," where the "center of gravity" of the person passes from the personality to the individuality, and where instinctive and natural egoism becomes conscious and voluntary altruism.

"Primitive persons" are driven and ruled by instincts or impulses. Such persons have not acquired self-knowledge or self-mastery, and remain subject to their primary needs. Biological survival is the crucial evolutionary task. At this level it is the "law of the jungle" that predominates. Suffering, pain, and fear are the masters and govern evolution. They learn by trial and error and pay for mistakes with physical pain.

"Ordinary persons" are driven and ruled primarily by emotions. They, too, do not have true knowledge and mastery of themselves to become the captain of their own ship and destiny. They are manipulated by others through their own emotions. Here, it is emotional survival that is essential. It is passionate and egoistical love—"falling in love"—that feels most real and important. The ordinary person feels controlled and shaped by society, their superiors, and the institutions to which they belong—family, church, work, and political party, for example. The center of their aspirations and primary values is to satisfy primary needs—eating, sleeping, having a family, affection, leisure, as well as material and emotional security.

"Talented persons" are driven and ruled by thoughts and the ego. They also do not have a real self-knowledge and self-mastery, but they think they have them. They think that, by reason and will, they can "make their way" in life, become an "important" person, and actualize themselves and their desires through competition. They always perceive life and society in dualistic terms: rich/poor, winners/losers, happy/unhappy persons. They have reached a certain actualization and integration of personality. They know what they want and know "effective" means to get it. They possess authentic talents and abilities, but remain egoistical and egocentric, ruled by the personality and its three primordial instincts: biological survival (linked with the first chakra), emotional survival (linked with the second chakra), and social/egoic survival (linked with the third chakra).

The talented person is one who has reached the maximum point of personal development, the culminating point of the personality wherein a person wants to know and to dominate society and the world to realize himself, and to live the good life on earth. It is the last stage before reaching the Great Passage, the true "Conversion"—the "death of the ego" and "birth of the Soul." It is in this category that we generally find political, economic, industrial, and religious leaders. It is also here that we can find the scientist, the artist, the physician, and the educator who have "made a name for themselves."

The authentic "Disciples" are those who have reached the opening of the fourth chakra, the opening of the Heart, and have gone beyond the center of attraction of the personality and of the human self (of the "earth") to enter under the center of attraction of the Soul and of the Spiritual Self, of the "Sun." These are the people who have lived or are living the true initiation, the death and resurrection, the total and radical transformation of their values, goals, and wills. And it is at this stage that every person will live the "to be or not to be" dilemma of Hamlet, in which everything must be reevaluated and redefined. We must decide to live through and for either the human or the Spiritual Self. It is also at this stage that one encounters the great crisis of personal identity: Who am I? Where do I come from and where am I going? Why have I come on earth and what must I do here? Finally, it is also here that the

true manifestation of God, "Revelation," or "Theopha
Up to this stage, human beings create gods in their ow
who change and transform with the expansion of their c
ness, as they are a function of the persons level of consc usness and being. Up to this stage, therefore, we really have idolatry, the confusion of reality with its image, and the projection of one's own ideas and phantasms upon reality. Up to this stage, religion can only be exoteric: God, tradition, and authority are apprehended and conceived as being exclusively outside rather than partly within oneself. Hence, up to this point, prayer remains intellectual, egoic, and self-centered; only beyond this point can it become spiritual (in the sense of "coming from the Self") and take on a living and effective nature. In other words, the Disciple dies to his own ego, to the phenomena, illusions, and charm of the world to be reborn to *noûmena*, to reality, where we are all "brothers" and "sisters," connected one to the other, and one in the deepest sense of this word.

It is perhaps because many people born at the end of W.W. II were able to enter the stage of the Disciple that we reached what has been termed the "age of anxiety," the "age of insecurity," the "age of the crisis of trust," with its near-total rejection of society and of the "establishment" by those who were struggling between the two basic influences: the personality and the individuality. They aspired to something better without being able to realize it. (The "hippies" were a good example of this.)

"Geniuses" are persons who function at the level of the fifth chakra and who have become the channels or instruments to manifest and radiate the Light and the Wisdom of God in the world, at least in part. Here thinking and reason reflect God's consciousness—or at least the higher consciousness—and no longer those of the human self, with its limited and egoic perceptions of the world and of the Self.

"Saints" are persons who function at the level of the sixth chakra and who have become the channels or instruments to manifest and radiate Spiritual Fire and the Love of God in the world. Here desires and emotions now reflect God consciousness, or at least the higher consciousness, and no longer those of the human self, with its limited and egoistic feelings and desires. The Love they express and radiate is a universal, impersonal, and efficacious love in the sense that it enables the loved ones to grow, to develop, to actualize their potentialities, and not to satisfy the caprices of their egos or to bring a temporary well-being based on gratified desires and wishes.

"Saints" truly radiate spiritual energies at their highest level, especially Love; these manifest as an inexhaustible source of healing, generosity, elevation, encouragement, and vivification for human beings in a world where true Love is rarer and more precious than gold. "True Masters" are extremely rare on our planet. They are persons who function at the level of the seventh chakra and who have become coordinated and perfected "temples" to manifest God's Will, the true Will of the Self—His Creative Energies—on earth. They are the only persons, on earth, who have succeeded in integrating perfectly Wisdom, Love, and Creative Energies in their own consciousness and being. It is in this way that they can act as the representatives and the transformers of the Divine Will, Energies, and Attributes in all the Worlds of Creation (or, at least, at the human level and on earth).

True Masters are the persons who know themselves and who have achieved the true control and mastery of their consciousness and being, and who are, therefore, fully reintegrated, having succeeded in completing their growth and in fulfilling their destiny on earth. Now, it is the Christ who thinks, feels, wills, speaks, and acts in them and through them. Liberated from the chains of destiny and of necessity, they are free to accomplish consciously and fully the mission they have chosen in this world and what God has entrusted to them. If they live for a certain period of time among us, it is because they have freely chosen and willed it—to accomplish tasks that Divinity has conferred upon them. They can incarnate and operate everywhere, in all races, countries, and cultures. They live the ordinary life of an ordinary person, all the while being permanently aligned with the Divine Light, the Fire, and the creative energies of the Spirit, which they manifest and radiate in the world. Like Jesus, who is their Archetype and Prototype in the world of matter, they represent and offer us a living model of the human being who has reached perfection and the complete realization of being, something which we shall all be one day, when we shall have completed our pilgrimage in the world of matter.

Once one truly grasps and understands the fundamental reality of different levels on the axis of consciousness one has an essential tool with which one can work upon and transform one's personality and the world. That is, instead of seeking for what is essential outside of one's self, in the world, in others, one can begin right away to look for it in one's self by purifying, consecrating, and uniting the field of consciousness with the Superconscious, the human with the spiritual Self. Then can we find God, the self, the ultimate reality, together with the true Masters, Teachers, or Superior Beings who will then appear to our consciousness and perceptions. For, should we not find them first within our selves, we will not find them in the world, where they do exist but where they remain ineluctably hidden, invisible, and silent.

To illustrate this idea of levels on the axis of consciousness, I would now like to give a few personal examples that led me to experience and appreciate this truth. Perhaps the greatest lessons that I have learned have come to me during periods of great crises in my life—that is, at times I least expected to learn something valuable. For example, a little after my twentieth birthday I went through a terrible motorcycle accident which left me half paralyzed and with many physical problems (pains, tensions, limitations) and psychological problems (depression, confusion, guilt, and frustration). Medical authorities, my family, and my friends all perceived and defined this situation as a "great catastrophe" and "a tragedy" for me. Hence, I too perceived and defined my situation as something dreadful, so that, in addition to my physical suffering and limitations, I also suffered a great deal psychologically. At a certain point, I even concluded that I had three basic choices: End my life, which then appeared to me as a long period of suffering and limitations as well as a heavy fiscal and psychological burden, for my family and my closest friends; continue to "vegetate" and to seek only to make my life as pleasant and secure as possible; or climb onto a higher level of consciousness which would hold the key to why this accident occurred to me and how I should "live it," or what I should now do with my life. Unconsciously at first, I began to adopt the perspective and to use the methods I had already learned from several persons that enable one to climb to a higher level of consciousness of being. And it was particularly through the regular use of prayer, physical exercise, and meditation, that I succeeded in climbing to a higher level, to a level at which I was able to reframe my situation, to accept it, and later, to heal slowly and fulfill the deep calling I felt swelling in the depths of my consciousness. This was the first time that I had experienced ascending or descending on the vertical axis of consciousness and felt its implications.

To describe this experience in symbolic language: I had found myself "in Hell," that is, in a state in which I suffered, physically and psychologically, in which I was depressed and asked myself why I had ended up in such a situation. What had I done to deserve this? And, What should I do about it? At the time, I had very little hope to heal and to have a better future. But, little by little, practicing prayer with great intensity, devotion, and concentration, I changed my state of being and my level of consciousness. Without being able truly to understand my situation, I succeeded in accepting it, in living with it, and in doing something valuable with my time, energies, and other resources. Thus, I read a great deal, I meditated, and I reflected. I met different types of people, some of whom helped me to reframe my situation and perceive it in a new light. I was living a spiritual test, a kind of initiation and, specifically, the "Earth Initiation" where the body is broken, where one has to accept handicaps and limitations of a physical nature.

Little by little, through prayer, I became consciously aware of the Light and of the Spiritual Energies which, when they manifested to my consciousness and "filled my being," brought me an undescribable energy and joy. My pains were diminishing and my strength was rising. One fine day, I became aware of the fact that my accident had forced me to look inside myself, to "ask Heaven for help," and to learn how to pray—that is, to draw down the Light so that my consciousness could expand and rise. In fact, without this accident, I wonder if I would have learned how to pray and to, thus, discover the Light and the Spiritual Energies. Thus my accident was transformed into a school for self-learning, into a marvelous opportunity to discover things that, otherwise, I would never have even dreamed of, and to acquire the most important skill of my life—conscious and living prayer.

From "Hell" I moved, little by little, with various ascents and descents, first to "Purgatory," and then eventually to "Heaven." What had been the worst catastrophe now became the greatest opportunity—an incredible trial and chance to learn and to live the greatest experience of my life to date. This experience helped me to relativize all human experiences and to understand that one can perceive and live them on very different levels and with very different meanings. I realized that, in the end, maybe all human experience, even the hardest and the most unjust, might well be a trial and an opportunity to discover, learn, and live things that are very important, even vital, for one's own evolution and for actualizing one's being.

After having lived this experience, I included prayer in my daily life and I continued praying, whether my life was easy or hard; but, I admit, more when things were hard, when I was in difficulty or in a state of crisis. Without realizing this or calling it by this name, I had discovered the possibility of changing one's consciousness by ascending or descending on the vertical axis of consciousness.

Thus, I learned that one can perceive, define, and react to any human situation in very different ways, which are a direct function of one's level of consciousness and being. Thus, by changing my level of consciousness I could radically change my perceptions, conceptions, definitions, and reactions to my situation. I could, in other words, move from hell to Earth, to Purgatory, and, finally, to Heaven: I could perceive this situation as a terrible catastrophe, reject it, and feel sorry for myself, suffering a great deal emotionally; *or* I could perceive this same situation as a great trial or spiritual initiation, accept it, do the best I could under the circumstances, and greatly diminish my psychological suffering.

I remember that, during the first days of another great test, I had to constantly guard and protect my heart (emotions), my imagination, and my thoughts, and especially, to pray as often as possible with the greatest fervor, lest I fall back to Hell where, again, I would greatly suffer. It even happened to me to pass from one state of mind to another, from Hell to Heaven within the space of half an hour. Moreover, I quickly learned (this time existentially and experimentally) that it was prayer, or a great concentration and projection of my attention, thoughts, and feelings towards the Superconscious and the Divine Spark, that acted as the buttons of an elevator to change my level of consciousness. In theory, I already knew this well, but now I was given a chance to personally live and experience this, which is something quite different. Now was imprinted upon my consciousness the fact that one can always, and almost immediately, change one's state of consciousness—climb to a higher floor—through work upon one's self and an expression of Love.

Paradoxically, it is when I was thrown into Hell that I experientially discovered the keys to Paradise and that I learned how to operate the "inner elevator" of the skyscraper, to move up and down the vertical axis of consciousness. And this is, perhaps, why it is said that to go to Heaven one must first experience the descent into Hell. Once one discovers, personally and experientially, this truth, then a universe of new possibilities and a sense of a great inner work opens to our awareness, giving new meaning and purpose to our lives on earth. For it is at this point, and at this point only, that one finally understands the great truth, repeated by many people but seldom truly understood, that *the key to reality, to our being, to life, love, and knowledge, as well as health and happiness, is to be found inside of ourselves.* And this key, at least for me, resides in the proper understanding and in the practical application of the insight contained in the vertical axis of consciousness.

One can wait for a major crisis before one discovers this fundamental key and begins to pray. But it is well to remember that one can also live through very serious crises without discovering and practicing prayer. The wisest and most prudent solution is to be prepared, to prepare oneself, that is, to enter the school of prayer and to begin the rewarding journey of a psychospiritual discipline. Because this is the way to truly open oneself fully to life, with all of its joys and sorrows, trials and adventures; to say a big "Yes" to life, without accepting the part that we find pleasant and rejecting the part we find unpleasant; and to live without fear.

It is the discovery and use of the philosopher's stone that

enables us to live without fear, and at the very heart of this stone we find the vertical axis of consciousness—expressed in words, symbols, and analogies that differ and change, but that always point to the same great truth. My hope and prayer is that you can make this truth your own, through your own efforts and experiences, and that it may exorcize, once and forever, the devil of fear, who can only live where there is no faith—and faith, of which we have spoken before, is a question of objectively changing your level of consciousness. You do not have to believe, gathering more data and beliefs quantitatively on the horizontal level you're on, but to change vertically to another level and experience Faith. Once you have lived this, life in all its complexity, diversity, and glory will be yours.

CHAPTER THREE

A Journey into the Inner Church: What a Student of the Mysteries Experiences in Church

Why do people go to church? What do they do while they are in church? And what are their expectations of a church service? Do students of the Mysteries go to church and, if so, why? How do they live the service?

Many go to church out of habit and custom, and not consciously as a journey into realms of spiritual consciousness. They go to church for traditional reasons: out of duty, to worship God, to humble themselves before the Creator, to give praise and thanksgiving. And, of course, this is right and good; but there can be lesser motivations: for example, because they had always been told to go to church and because they were taken there by their parents. Thus, a habit forms which has a natural tendency to continue. Others go to church for social reasons: there are people in church they want to see and who want to see them. Should they not go, they might feel they are letting down their clergy, parents, children, friends, or neighbors. Others go to church for emotional reasons: singing together, to hear the sermon, or to participate in the liturgy, which gives them a generally good overall feeling. The liturgy might also help them release their emotions and their thoughts from mundane anxieties and desires; it enables them to have "quiet moments," to reflect on some important issue, and to send thoughts of love to dear ones. Finally, they might go to church as a "death insurance," just in case there is a Soul that might, somehow, benefit from church services. In all these cases, many who go to church do not put a great deal of themselves into the experience and therefore do not get much from it. Thus, they might not go to church a few times, or even for a long period of their lives.

For a student of the Holy Wisdom, and even more for an Initiate of the Mysteries, the situation is very different. First, and foremost, they go to church consciously or, more precisely put, in growing and unfolding degrees of consciousness. They also know from experience that they will receive a hundredfold what they gave of themselves. For them, it is not tradition, social, emotional, mental, or socio-cultural reasons, or a vague "death insurance," that brings them to church; rather, it is a response to the beckoning of the Most High, who sets before us at this banquet many gifts and goals and holy objects that we can meet, comprehend, and experience with the fullness of our being and consciousness. As Evelyn Underhill appropriately declares:

> The conviction that religious experience is to be taken as the starting-point of theological reconstruction does not, of course, imply that we are absolved from the labor of thought. On the contrary, it should serve as the stimulus for thought. No experience can be taken at its face value; it must be criticized and interpreted . . . as Mazzini finely said: "Tradition and conscience are the two wings given to the human soul to reach the truth." . . .
>
> Worship is here considered in its deepest sense, as the response of man to the Eternal: and when we look at the many degrees and forms of this response, and the graded character of human religion, its slow ascent from primitive levels and tendency to carry with it the relics of its past, we need not be surprised that even within the Christian family there is much diversity in the expressive worship which is yet directed towards a single revelation of the Divine.[1]

Thus will the student of the Mysteries approach a church service for healing and enlightenment, to commune with God, both as the Other and as the Higher Self, to obtain a direct experience of the Divine Light and Fire, of Divine Life that can be infused even into one's very blood—an experience that runs through one's entire being, from the spiritual to the physical level. Here is the place of spiritual interaction that will bring a life more abundant and that will immediately and directly transform one's consciousness and state of being, so that thinking, feeling, and willing are illuminated, transformed, consecrated, and vivified. If only for a brief moment, we find and are united with our Divine Spark, the Christ within.

They go to church to feed their Soul with the Divine Light, which has the effect of activating the intuition, clarifying the mind, purifying and intensifying the emotions, and raising the level of energy and vitality available to body and psyche. They go to church and participate in the service to practice regularly a most important part of the Great Work known as *worship. Worship* implies to consciously climb the Sacred Mountain of the Superconscious, where God dwells and will appear to them, where they will obtain a revelation, a theophany, that will enable them better to carry out the other fundamental aspect of the great work, which is living daily life in a more conscious, productive, creative, and joyful fashion. And, seen from this perspective, what could be more important and more life-giving than going to church?

When a student of the Holy Wisdom, or an Initiate of the Mysteries goes to church, his or her first awareness can be that here one enters the temple of one's own consciousness, that here one works not solely in the world but deeply in one's own Soul. The student brings this conscious sense of worship and spiritual work from the fullness of his or her life experience and spiritual training, which, we hope, will now also include a direct and conscious working with the psychospiritual centers of his or her Tree of Life and with the energy-fields or auras, as we have called them before. One can begin the preparation either at home, before going to church, or in the church itself, where the atmosphere and the conditions might be more conducive to that preparation. For present purposes, we will assume that the preparation is done in church rather than before.

Structurally and functionally, the initiate goes through a threefold preparation, transformation, or *metanoia*, to purify and consecrate her mental, emotional, and vital bodies. With her mind, she must first have an over-all understanding and perspective concerning what she is doing and why she is doing what she is doing. Emotionally, she must really open up, direct, and consecrate her heart and feelings to what she is doing. Finally, with her will, she needs to direct all her attention to what is at hand and achieve the highest level of concentration possible.

At the mental level, she prepares with the realization that she is about to enter a vital and indispensable part of the Great Work called worship or communion with God as well as with the Higher Self. The candidate must realize that the whole service is a gradual preparation, which culminates in the Eucharist or Communion. Then, she will have to decode, interpret, or directly intuit spiritually on her level of consciousness the images, words, and actions that she will find in the church and in the service so that they may become alive and meaningful in her own consciousness. As the spiritual tradition puts it succinctly: "It is by Name and Images that all Powers are awakened and reawakened." This means, for example, that one can see in the physical church of wood and stone a representation of the inner anatomy and physiology of the Soul, of the Tree of Life, with all its psychospiritual centers. This means that entering the church, one also enters into the inner temple, or aura, to begin the slow ascent on the Tree of Life leading to the heart, which is represented by the altar.

The entrance to the church, or the doorway furthest from the altar where most people enter, represents on the Tree of Life *Malkuth*, the physical, telluric Feet Center; *Tippherethr*, the psychic, human Heart Center, corresponds to the altar; and the dome or rose-window above or behind the altar, represents *Kether*, the Cosmic Head Center. The candidate must realize that the whole service is a stage of gradual preparation that culminates in the Eucharist or Communion. This symbolic representation of working with the Tree of Life and the psychospiritual centers offers a practical means to awaken, activate, and achieve an altered state of consciousness, the raised vibrations and energies of which will allow for a true communion to occur between the human and the spiritual Self, the field of consciousness and the Superconscious.

At the emotional level, the Heart Center is to be opened so that she can pour all her feelings and emotions into each separate part of the service so that it is not only understood but felt. Though basically simple, yet hard to describe, this step is vital and indispensable. For without the life-giving warmth of the heart, all the mental meditation and practical activities, and all the concentration and affirmations of the will, remain purely psychological and therefore sterile in activating the spiritual transfusion and transformation which is the essence of this whole process. As Dion Fortune declares:

> Desire is prayer. When we desire a thing, we are invoking as far as lies in our power and a great deal more lies in our power than we realize though its manifestations are not always seen in the immediate future.[2]

At the level of the will, she must be able to really concentrate all her attention, thoughts, feelings, and energies upon what she is doing, avoiding all distractions and dissipations. This, too, is a most important step, which is hard to describe, and which can only really be learned by experience and by doing it. Evelyn Underhill explains, quoting Richard of St. Victor:

> Richard of St. Victor has said, that the essence of all purification is self simplification: the doing away of all unnecessary and unreal, the tangles and complications of consciousness. The pure soul is like a lens from which all irrelevancies and excrescences, all the beams and motes of egotism and prejudice have been removed; so that it may reflect a clear image of the one Transcendent.[3]

And she concludes:

> The dynamic power of love and will, the fact that the Heart's desire—if it be intense and industrious—is a better earnest of possible fulfillment than the most elegant theories of the spiritual world; this is the perpetual theme of all the Christian mystics. By such love, they think, the worlds themselves are made.[4]

When the Initiate enters through the Door of the Church, the focus of awareness can be as follows:

1. Realize that they are entering the temple of their own inner consciousness, of the Soul, at the level of Malkuth, or the Feet Center. And this, in turn, means—
   a. To bring about a threefold consciousness-transformation involving the magical, hermetic, and alchemical traditions; consciously moving from space to sacred space,

from profane time to sacred time, and from profane events to sacred events. This transformation is volitional, mental, and emotional.

b. Thus, there is a directed effort of introversion, withdrawing attention and psychic energies from the outside world to refocus them on the inside world—on one's field of consciousness.
c. One must consciously let go of the past and of the future, of pet fears and anxieties, as well as of one's most pressing desires and aspirations, to become as emotionally and mentally centered and focused on the present as is possible.
d. Realize and reaffirm that the task at hand is the single most important and vital work one can do—a vital part of the Great Work.

2. Then, walk up the nave, or central aisle, representing the Middle Pillar of Consciousness, choosing a pew towards the right aisle, representing the Right Pillar of Form, or towards the left aisle, symbolizing the Left Pillar of Force. One may also select a place closer or further away from the altar, representing the Heart Center, according to one's present state of consciousness and the energies and vibrations one is trying to awaken and work with at this point. Thus, concretely speaking, we can sit and "center" ourself at the level of *Yesod* (the Sexual Center), *Hod* (the Right Hip Center), or *Netzach* (the Left Hip Center) and visualize ourself in such a position, activating the corresponding center on our own inner Tree of Life.
3. Finally, the student should visualize the rest of the tree, awakening and activating its corresponding Centers in his own consciousness and aura, by focusing at the head of the left aisle with the blue candle light, symbolizing *Chesed,* with the Blue-clad Madonna behind it, corresponding to the female aspect of *Chockmah.* Then, he should focus at the head of the right aisle with the red candle light, symbolizing *Geburah,* with the red-clad St. Joseph behind it, corresponding to the male aspect of *Binah.* Finally, he should focus on the Altar and the Dome, or Rose-Window behind it,

representing, respectively, the Heart Center of *Tippherethand* the Head Center of *Kether.*

In conclusion, you, as an aspirant of the Mysteries, a student in Christian initiation, can do the same. You can, in other words, "walk through" and then activate your own *Malkuth, Yesod,* and *Netzach,* according to where you decide to sit and the kind of work you wish to accomplish on that day. Finally, you should complete your visualization internally of *Tippheret h, Geburah, Chesed, Binah, Chockmah,* and *Kether.* If you are a purist and stick to the details, you literally will have walked through (signifying having activated) the centers up to the one you will be sitting in. Then work from this particular center while visualizing those centers that lie ahead of you, which remain to be activated in the future.

At some point early in the Mass, the priest may go through a formula of collective confession, penance, and absolution, or he may not. But you, as an aspirant Initiate, should personally go through these in your own Temple and Consciousness as they deal with fundamental aspects of the progressive purification at the mental, astral, and vital levels. This implies going through an exam of conscience. Conduct a careful analysis in the present of the seven functions of your psyche in your own field of consciousness. This helps to check how well your powers of concentration, meditation, devotion, visualization, invocation-evocation, energy direction and transmutation, and inner observation are working at present. Do any of these functions and processes need to be cleansed, intensified, or coordinated with the others? Then go over briefly the events of the last week, last month, or whatever the period of time since you last did this, to call to mind what you did that violates your conscience, as well as what you wanted to do but did not do. Then, take up these materials, sins, or errors of commission and omission, bring them into your consciousness, make a resolve to rectify them as soon as you can, and then release them into the forgiving Light of Christ, both within as the spiritual Self and without. This process helps to purify your aura at the mental, emotional, and vital levels, to cleanse and unclog your psychospiritual centers at the conscious or unconscious level. Negative thoughts, feelings, desires, words, and deeds do affect and change the aura and the centers. They bring or evoke negative energies, colors, and vibrations. This clogs up the centers, lowers your vibrations, consciousness, and vitality, and creates a cloud or barrier that prevents the spiritual light and energies from descending and operating in your field of consciousness and personality. Moreover, these have three specific death-bringing impacts upon your consciousness, diminishing it, lowering it, and confusing it (for greater details, see the chapter on the Sacraments, the sections on Penance and Absolution in *Divine Light and Fire*), namely:

a. They confuse the mind so that one is no longer able to think clearly and to distinguish what is good from what is bad, what we should and should not do. The mental confusion and amnesia that ensue are analogous to what happens when we turn off the light in a room without windows: we no longer see anything, but can only grope in darkness.
b. They harden the heart and erode our capacity to feel anything positive and beautiful, making us either insensitive or filled up with negative feelings of fear, guilt, insecurity, and despair. Here, it is the Heart Center which is directly affected, clogged up, and poisoned so that our capacity to be ourselves, to love, and to live is blocked and replaced by negative emotional explosions and ups and downs. It is as if all life and love went out from our heart to be replaced by a burning sense of frustration, anxiety, anger, insecurity, guilt, unattainable desires and longings, and despair.
c. They sap and deplete the energies of the will until one loses control over the functions of the psyche: one's thoughts, feelings, vitality, words, deeds and ultimately, over one's whole life and being. Without will and without self, one drifts through life, pushed here and there, by emotional currents, a victim of circumstances, helplessly sinking deeper and deeper into lethargy and apathy, into self-amnesia and into anti-social, even self-destructive, behavior.

The final psychological and existential results of this process, which can manifest to any degree are depression and despair (the former being a great "enigma" of modern medicine, the roots of which are psychospiritual in nature).

Having opened up the unconscious and dredged up the demons of the depths and of the past, the second part of this process consists in bringing down the Light and the Energies of the Divine Spark into the field of consciousness, to transform and transmute them. To achieve this result, the candidate can now visualize a beautiful Sphere of Light above and around his Head Center, then call down and draw in a ray of its Light, and thus its Energies, into the Heart Center, where the field of consciousness is now located and where the demons of the depths and of the past have been summoned.

This basic visualization can be followed by a prayer. The one I use is this:

> Oh Heavenly Father, unto Thee do I turn, in this tiny temple of my consciousness, to thank You for the great Gift of Life, of Love, and of Self-expression, and for the countless opportunities and tests to grow that You are providing for me. I confess that I have sinned against Thee in thought, in word, and in deed; that I have not loved You as much as I could have loved You; and that I did not have the faith in You that I should have had but, rather, that I have let myself fall prey to lower states of consciousness—of thinking, feeling, willing, speaking, and acting; that I have been selfish, lazy, and apathetic, and have wasted my energies and opportunities to grow and to serve Thee and my fellow humans.

And here, of course, you can put in those mistakes of commission or omission you feel you have committed during that period of time. I then conclude with:

> But now with repentance and contrition, I turn again to Thy mercy and I beseech Thee to grant me forgiveness for all of my sins, whether known to me, or unknown, in thought, word, and deed, in the Name of the Father, and of the Son, and of the Holy Spirit. May the power of Thine all Holy Spirit grant me absolution for all my sins. Amen. Amen. Amen.

It is the Names of Power of the Holy Trinity, used with the Sign of the Cross, that actually carries out this "alchemical" purification and which transforms the energies, vibrations, and colors of the Head, Heart, and Shoulder Centers which, in turn, affect the whole Aura, the other Centers, and the level of consciousness. This concludes the preparation.

The liturgy or Mass follows the fundamental sequence of purification, consecration, and unification.

Purification is the basic alchemical transformation of our state of consciousness: thoughts, feelings, and vitality; the raising of our vibratory rate, the cleansing of the psychospiritual Centers, and the opening up of Jacob's Ladder, the channel between the Superconscious and the conscious, between the spiritual world and ourselves.

Consecration is the focusing and use of all of one's faculties and energies for the work at hand, by our effort and God's grace "making ourselves and being made holy" in the process of psychospiritual transformation and communion with the higher Self and with the Superconscious.

Unification is the descent of the Divine Light and the alignment of the spiritual Self with the human self, of the Superconscious with the conscious, of Christ with the candidate (or his soul). (For greater details see the chapter on the Roman Catholic Mass.)

This very central process involves deliberately transforming our consciousness, energies, and vibrations, manifesting through our thoughts, feelings, desires, word, and deeds. It involves taking the elevator and raising our center of consciousness to the higher floors of our being, or slowly ascending on the Holy Mountain where the Divine Light, Fire, and Life of Christ can consciously manifest and descend into our being. Thus, we raise our consciousness and evoke the Divine Light and Fire, which can then further raise and transform our consciousness, changing our very perceptions of reality and our identity, aligning our will with His.

What the priest does at the altar and in the church, the candidate must reproduce and mirror in his own heart and aura. What matters is not the external actions we are to reproduce, but what we can bring to these through our inner gestures; our attitude, which can unite with the gestures of the ritual or ceremony. Once again, it is not what the priest does at the altar, or the candidate in his Heart, that is the operational key, but the faith the candidate applies to his inner work.

Upon entering the church, the candidate will walk across the center aisle and bow or genuflect before the altar, tracing the sign of the Cross upon himself, being aware of what preparation is to be done, also absorbing and incorporating the Light and energies that the two angels at the altar are radiating (projected through the male and female polarities). The candidate, then, has to become of aware of participating both externally and internally in the service; singing the various songs and making the appropriate responses, giving attention to what is outside of himself, but also following the service inwardly, following the inward rhythm, leading to his own inner worlds. Experiencing both the outer and the inner, the objective and the subjective, is, I feel, the most productive approach. Thus, at times, the candidate will really "get into" his or her own world through an intense effort of concentration and consciousness transformation, while at other times, he or she will follow the external service so as best to reproduce it within, now or at a later time.

All the words said by the priest must be used theurgically by the candidate so as to make them become his own inner reality. Thus, whatever the priest is saying the candidate will repeat within himself; every word must thus awaken, within his field of consciousness, the powers, energies, vibrations, and materials to which they correspond. And he must first know these materials, then feel them, and finally, incarnate them. This is the true key of all rituals, which in a living way reconnect us with inner and outer reality. It is also what will enable the candidate to literally enter into another world, the inner world of the psyche, where both Heaven and Hell exist and can be experienced as powerful, real, and living forces.

The Divine Liturgy, or Mass, is the one practical and completely psychospiritual exercise to be practiced weekly in the "laboratory" of the external temple, and in the inner temple of our consciousness, or aura. The Mass, or church service, can be seen as a trinity with a body, a soul, and a spirit. The body is the best known and most obvious "empirical" part: it is the physical building of the temple or church and the physical words and deeds of the Liturgy. The soul is the explanation of the meaning, the implications and applications, of the service. It is a function of the level of consciousness of the participant, and differs with the different levels of being. Hence, the soul is the truly human, dynamic, growing, unfolding, emergent level, where there is most often a direct relationship between what we do and what we receive.

Generally, the soul of any religion or ritual can be subdivided into two basic aspects, which we have described before: the exoteric and the esoteric. The exoteric aspect is the external one, or the "letter," handed down through human history, cautiously refined and given official approbation; it is the one in which we are asked to take a more receptive position, to examine present truth, principles, rituals, ceremonies, etc. in light of tradition in which, while based on direct experience, faith plays the larger part. The exoteric aspect can also refer to that which corresponds to the collective consciousness of the majority of members of a community at any given time. This aspect also changes with time, but with judicious slowness, as opposed to the dynamics, and the candor and courage of the esoteric aspect.

The esoteric aspect is the internal one, or the "spirit," the one we can work to discover by our own efforts, growth, and transformation of consciousness. It is the one where the external, physical events and processes have to be internalized in terms of our own psyche, soul and spiritual development, in the microcosm that is our consciousness. More primarily, it is the realm of the direct, personally lived experience of the sacred or of the Mysteries. In the present chapter, our central focus has been the esoteric aspect of going to church and of participating in the Mass as derived from the knowledge and lived experience of the author.

The exoteric aspect is well-defined and accessible, and can be found by going to a church, reading in the tradition and the liturgy, attending catechism, or asking questions of members of the clergy. The esoteric aspect, on the other hand, must ultimately be discovered and experienced by oneself—though a number of spiritually awakened and creative people have written and spoken about it.

Finally, the Spirit is the Light, Fire, and Life—the energies, vibrations, and powers—that stand behind the external church and its rituals. It is the source whence they came and the end for which they were instituted. As a candidate expands his level of consciousness by degrees and raises his level of being, he is led by the rituals of the Church from the outer to the inner, from the "letter" to the "spirit." But what Spirit is fundamentally can only be personally experienced in silence, in that most intimate of experiences known as Communion, in which the Spirit informs and transforms the soul and body.

The central purpose in developing this chapter is simply to inspire you, the candidate: to motivate you and to get you to participate more and more consciously and fully in the service you attend, especially the Mass. It aims to enable you to draw greater and greater benefits from it, to make it come alive in your consciousness, and to enable you to achieve a conscious and experiential contact and "communion" with that source whence all light, love, and life come and whence alone you can find the true answers to the most fundamental questions of your life and being.

The central purpose in developing this or any other ritual is so that it can reveal its mysteries to you, and thus accomplish its purpose: to make you come alive and fulfill *your* true purpose in this world. The emphasis is thus not on what is being said and done, but on *how* it is being said and done, on what you bring to it as you are going through it. Faith, in this regard, can be seen as a **trinity**; the trinity of thinking, feeling, and willing—of meditation, devotion, and concentration, of pouring upon a point all of your human knowledge, human love, and human will. Thus can this service be understood, experienced, and rendered more effective for you when you participate in it as fully and as consciously as possible. The service cannot be a solo operation or a clergy operation, it has to become a "together operation" in which you will pour all your heart, mind, and soul. In this way, the Church, and its weekly service, though there are many profound and exalted meanings and approaches, can also become a true inner and outer psychospiritual "laboratory" to practice and achieve the following:

1. Exercise and train the seven functions of the psyche: willing, thinking, feeling, intuition, imagination, biopsychic drives, and sensations.
2. Practice, develop, and coordinate the psychological processes related to the seven functions of the psyche:
   Concentration: focusing all of one's attention upon a given subject;

Meditation: organizing all of one's knowledge and understanding about a given subject and then being inspired to learn more;
Devotion: awakening and pouring one's feeling and love into a given subject;
Visualization: reproducing on the screen of one's mind external images, colors, and events in their appropriate representation;
Invocation-Evocation: making a human effort to converge the four foregoing functions upon a point so as to open one's self to a descent and infusion of Light and inspiration;
Energy Direction and Transformation: transmuting lower and unbalanced forces into higher and more balanced ones, and harnessing the vitality and energy thus released;
Inner Observation: learning how to look at, become aware of, and study one's stream of awareness and its transformations.

3. Attunement, dialogue internally, and commune with the higher Self, the Christ within; creating a Ladder of Jacob or "channel" between the Superconscious and the conscious, the spiritual and the human self, so that the Divine Light, Fire, and Life of Christ may consciously pour forth into our awareness, being, and Life to truly regenerate us, redeem us, and make us *whole*.

The truly fundamental question of life is how to achieve the union with God, or how to reconnect ourselves consciously with the Source and Essence of all Life, Love, and Wisdom in a way that satisfies the deepest longings and aspirations of our higher nature. The Church and especially the Mass are a practical inner/outer psychospiritual laboratory wherein a living transformative process can occur, leading the participant to achieve progressive self-knowledge, self-mastery, and self-integration—the threefold goals of the Great Work, leading to this one fundamental goal of union.

The basic esoteric keys that can be given, but which must be personally experienced, are that the Church, in one way (at least in terms of this approach) can be seen as an analogue of your aura, the Tree of Life with its Centers, and an external representation of your soul. The priest, then, represents your will and your reason, your conscious self. The altar corresponds to your heart center and the Sanctuary, a higher state of consciousness—which is why the Orthodox Church, a more mystical Christian Church, always has an Iconoclasia, a row of Icons between the Temple (ordinary consciousness) and the Sanctuary (a higher state of consciousness).

For it is in the Sanctuary of your higher consciousness, on the Altar of your Heart, that your will and reason, aided by your imagination and intuition, must seek to bring down the downpouring of Divine Light, Fire, and Life. Thus, you can take each prayer and petition, said by the Priest, focus upon it, repeat it, and make it come alive in your consciousness, so that it will awaken and elicit those Energies, Powers, and Vibrations to which it corresponds. Then, let all your ideas, feelings, intuitions, and images gather and flow around it so as to awaken and bring down new life, thoughts, feelings, intuitions, and visions. Let your consciousness fuse with them, become them, and live them so that they may become "flesh in you," that is thought-forms, inner realities, and doors to higher consciousness and realizations.

The immediate objectives of the Catholic Mass and the Orthodox Liturgy is *achieving conscious union with God, with the Divine Spark within, which is Spiritual Initiation.* This implies to "heal the sick," both within and without oneself; to "enlighten the ignorant"; and to become whole, to reintegrate consciously all the parts of the self, and of the self with reality, with God, nature, and other human beings.

Every time we go to Church, participate in a religious service, and take Communion, we move a little closer to achieving consciously these grand objectives. *Healing, enlightenment,* and *wholeness,* these are the three fundamental components of *Salvation.* And to achieve these, in turn, three distinct operations and phases are required:

First, **Purification:** the cleansing of the mental, emotional, and vital "bodies" and the progressive "unclogging" of the psychospiritual Centers, to align the personality with the soul so that your vibrations, consciousness, and energies may be raised and harmonized.

Second, **Consecration:** utilizing all the functions of the psyche, all the energies and materials of our Centers, and focusing our whole attention upon the work at hand so as to reawaken and synthesize our consciousness to that part of our being and to energize our consciousness for the final part of this process.

Third, **Communion:** the actual interaction and exchange between the human and the spiritual selves, the conscious and the Superconscious, the human and the Divine, and the breakthrough of the Divine Light, Fire, and Life of the Divine Spark into our consciousness. Here, the Body of Christ and the Blood of Christ, mysteriously present in the bread and wine, convey to us the Divine Light and Fire, attuning our consciousness to that source of all consciousness and love. Within us, the Divine Light and Fire engender *spiritual life,* raising and transforming our vibrations, consciousness, and energies. And the result of this cannot be described in words but only experienced: something that could be called "ecstasy," the deepest, most intense and joyful human experience. (For more on this experience, please see as well the section on the Eucharist in the chapter on the Sacraments in *Divine Light and Fire.*

As Evelyn Underhill writes in her eloquent style:

> "Going forth in the bareness and darkness of this unwalled world of high contemplation, you there find stored for you, and at last made real, all the highest values, all the dearest and noblest experiences of the world of growth and change. You see now what it is that you have been doing in the course of your mystical development. As your narrow heart stretched to a wider sympathy with life, you have been surrendering progressively to larger and larger existences, more and more complete realities: have been learning to know them, to share their very being, through the magic of disinterested love. First the manifested, flowing, evolving life of multiplicity: felt by you in its wonder and wholeness, once you learned to yield yourself to its rhythms, received in simplicity the distorted messages of sense. Then, the actual unchanging ground of life, the eternal and unconditional Whole, transcending all succession: a world inaccessible alike to senses and intelligence, but felt—vaguely, darkly, yet intensely—by the quiet and surrounded consciousness. But now you are solicited, whether you will or not, by a greater Reality, the final inclusive Fact, the Unmeasured

Love, which "is responding to its obscure yet ardent communications, you pass beyond the cosmic experience to the *personal encounter,* the simple yet utterly inexpressible union of the soul with its God."[5]

CHAPTER FOUR

The Role of Prayer in Esoteric Christianity

Prayer is not another means or psychospiritual technology to bring special favors from God or to get what our human self wants; neither is it a way to get out of desperate straits when all else fails, nor a way to satisfy a religious duty, or to do good in this world to earn credits in the next world. Prayer is a primary way to expand and change our consciousness so that we can know the will of God and do it, in our own being and life. It is a way to know and understand more of what we could not know or understand before. It is a way to receive more energy or life force, so that we can do or carry out what we are meant to in the precise and specific situation in which we find ourselves. When we know and understand better what is happening to us, we experience an increase and intensification of our creative energies, or vitality, so that we can then do it. Finally, we acquire that deep inner peace, that feeling of gratitude for being given the opportunity to learn valuable lessons, and we realize the joy of being alive, knowing who we are, what we are meant to do, and being able to do it.

For our physical body to be healthy, to function and to grow into maturity and serve as our multidimensional vehicle of expression, it must be properly fed by the right combination of nutrients at the right time and in the right mix and measure; for the biological organism is largely the product of what we eat. Analogously, our human consciousness, the various energy bodies that act as its matrix, and its basic functions must also be fed and properly nourished. And it is human exchanges that constitute the food, fuel, or nourishment of our consciousness. Thus, to think, to feel, to will—to use our intuition, imagination, and to express our biopsychic drives and our sensations—we must interact with others to receive the proper nourishment. (For more on biopsychic drives in the functioning of the human psyche, see Appendix A.) Without this, our consciousness would starve and slowly fade into unconsciousness, and we would become "strangers to ourselves" and "aliens" in an incomprehensible, indifferent, or hostile world. We become depressed, worn out, confused, bored, frustrated, and victims of circumstance, unable to be and to express ourselves. For just as the physical body needs to be fed, so our energy bodies also need to be fed.

The same analogy applies on the soul-level—on the higher levels and expressions of our being and of our consciousness. The soul, too, must "eat" and be properly fed, and prayer is its "food"—the Divine Light, Fire, and Life of the spiritual energies, which are invoked and evoked, brought into our field of consciousness, and circulated in our consciousness and being. Without this "food," regularly taken and properly assimilated, the soul consciousness will fade away—or fall asleep, for the soul cannot die. Once awakened, the soul or higher consciousness must be fed through prayer or disappear—to the point that many people even question the existence of this consciousness, not to mention its expression. Thus, the maxim: Feed yourself, that is, all the "bodies" which are vehicles of expressing yourself, or die on many levels.

It is this that explains the great paradox of prayer; namely, that for some it is meaningless and useless, while for others it is the "food of their soul" and the most important activity in which they can engage. This is also why praying awakens the desire to pray more and more often, as will the absence of prayer annul the desire and the felt need to pray.

Prayer, like other fundamental activities and expressions, is a function of our level of consciousness and being. Above a certain level and threshold of consciousness it becomes clearly and consciously an essential activity, while below a certain level and threshold of consciousness it becomes manifestly incomprehensible and seemingly worthless. Thus, for some it can seem merely a dead traditional or mental exercise, one which is perhaps only carried out mechanically to satisfy one's religious conscience, duty, or habits; while for others it literally accomplishes miracles, both in one's consciousness and in the world. And between these two there are all degrees of experience.

It is in praying that we discover the true nature, meanings, implications, and applications, the mysteries and treasures, of prayer just as it is said that in doing one becomes a master of what is being done. The French have a proverb, applicable on many different levels: "C'est en forgeant qu'on devient forgeron": it is in forging that one becomes a blacksmith. It is your own personal experiences and results that will really teach you about the esoteric aspects and treasures of prayer. All I can do, or others can do, is to reach your mind, heart, and will to motivate you to do the work, to become involved in living prayer and discover its great treasures and power. And this is what all the sacred traditions and the great religions do and have done, in more or less explicit, clear or symbolic, terms.

Evelyn Underhill summarizes the process of "awakening to spiritual consciousness," which is what prayer is about, in the following words:

> The education of the mystical sense begins in self-simplification. The feeling, willing, seeing self is to move from the various and the analytical to the simple and the synthetic . . . The essence of mystical contemplation is summed up in these two experiences—union with the flux of life and union with the Whole in which all the lesser realities are resumed—and these experiences are well within your reach . . . You are already in fact a potential contemplative: for this act, St. Thomas Aquinas taught, is proper to all men—is, indeed, the characteristic human activity.[1]

This raises more specific questions about prayer, such as:

1. What is prayer? What constitutes its essential nature?
2. What are the basic and specific functions of prayer? What can prayer do?
3. What are some of the most important prayers in our own Christian tradition?
4. What makes prayer become alive and effective? How can one go from the "letter" to the "spirit" of prayer so that it can bring about immediate transformations in our consciousness?

5. What is the essential secret of prayer?
6. What preliminary training and discipline can be used to make prayer become alive and effective in our own consciousness and life?
7. How can one organize one's self and one's life to include a "healthy dose" of prayer, used daily and regularly, as well as in crisis situations and, especially, before making a crucial decision or embarking in a new "adventure" or direction in our lives?

1. What is prayer and what constitutes its essential nature?

All kind of conceptions and definitions of "prayer" have emerged over the centuries. One I have recently heard in America, and which distinguishes "prayer" from "meditation," is the following: "prayer is speaking to God, whereas meditation is listening to God speaking to us." Prayer is a form of inner dialogue, of communications and exchanges between ourselves and God and the cosmos, as well as between the parts of ourselves. It is the conscious effort to connect our field of consciousness with our Superconscious, our human self with the spiritual Self, with the Divine Spark, and through the Divine Spark and our Superconscious to connect ourselves and to communicate, in a "telepathic" fashion, as it were, with the cosmic God. Seen in another way, it is the "royal way" to expand our consciousness, to, at least temporarily, climb the sacred mountain of our Superconscious wherein we may commune with the Divine Light, Fire, and Life. It is a way to raise our field of consciousness to higher levels on our inner axis of consciousness and being. Finally, as I have pointed out before, it is a way to feed and nourish our Soul with its own form of nutrients. It is thus a fundamental way to find our self and commune with Him.

Just as we have to eat physical food to nourish our biological organism, as we have to interact with other human beings to "feed our consciousness" (our energy bodies) so prayer is a way to "nourish our Soul" . . . and to do this in a regular and periodic way.

It is true that many people do not pray and do not feel any need or desire to pray, though I believe that all human beings will develop this emergent need and desire. A person who functions solely on the level of the personality—that is, on the sensory, emotional and mental level—may not pray, not understand what prayer is really all about, and therefore experiences no need or desire to pray; but as soon as that person "pierces through" or reaches the Soul level, or when that person goes through a very deep and "shattering" (that is, "disorienting and disorganizing") crisis, or when this same person falls deeply and profoundly in love, then this "new" need and desire will emerge in an imperative way. Thus, we should not criticize people for not praying if they do not feel this need, but we can tell them and explain to them what prayer really is, what its true functions and deeper purpose really are. And, in their own time, or in the time of their Divine Spark, they will feel the need and the desire to find out more about prayer and to put it to work in their own consciousness and lives.

Thus, I would say that prayer is not so much something that we can talk about as something that we can feel, experience, and live, something that will teach us more about itself through practicing it than through reading about it, taking lectures or workshops, or speculating about its true nature and role in our lives. One thing is certain: anyone who has ever prayed in an alive and authentic way will have the greatest appreciation and respect for what prayer is and what prayer can do. To underscore this, I would like to cite the words of the Nobel Laureate and medical doctor Alexis Carrell:

> . . . Prayer is not only worship; it is also an invisible emanation of man's worshiping spirit—the most powerful form of energy that one can generate. If you make a habit of sincere prayer, your life will be very noticeably and profoundly enriched. Prayer is a force as real as terrestrial gravity. As a physician, I have seen men, after all other therapy has failed, lifted out of disease and melancholy by the serene effort of prayer. Such occasions have been termed "miracles." But a constant quieter "miracle" takes place hourly in the hearts of men and women who have discovered that prayer supplies them with a steady flow of sustaining power in their daily lives.
>
> Too many people regard prayer as a formalized routine of words, a refuge for weaklings or a childish petition for material things. Properly understood, prayer is a mature activity indispensable to the fullest development of personality. Only in prayer do we achieve that

complete and harmonious assembly of body, mind, and spirit which gives the frail human reed its unshakable strength.

. . . How does prayer fortify us with so much dynamic power? To answer this question (admittedly outside the jurisdiction of science), I must point out that all prayers demonstrate the same truth: human beings seek to augment their finite energy by addressing themselves to the infinite source of all energy. When we pray, we link ourselves with the inexhaustible motive power that spins the universe. We ask that a part of this power be appropriated to our needs. Even in asking, our human deficiencies are filled, and we arise strengthened and repaired.

. . . In order to really mold personality, prayer must become a habit. One can pray everywhere; in the streets, in the office, the school, the solitude of one's room, in a church. There is no prescribed posture, time or place. But it is meaningless to pray in the morning and to live like a barbarian the remainder of the day. True prayer is a way of life; the truest life is literally a way of prayer.

Today, lack of emphasis on the religious has brought the world to the edge of destruction. Our deepest source of power and perfection has been left miserably undeveloped. Prayer, the basic exercise of the spirit, must be actively practiced by men and nations. For if the power of prayer is again released and used in the lives of common men and women, if the spirit declares its aims clearly and boldly, there is yet hope that our prayers for a better world will be answered.[2]

2. What are the basic and specific functions of prayer? What can prayer do?

If one is to invest attention, time, energy, and effort to develop a meaningful, regular prayer life, then it is most important that one understands not only what prayer is, what constitutes its "essential nature" but also and especially what the core functions of prayer are—what prayer can and cannot do for a person. Unfortunately, a great deal of confusion, misinformation, illusions, and superstitions (older truths and principles that have become fragmented, misinterpreted, and distorted) exist concerning prayer. To begin with, let me state emphatically that prayer is not an "inner," "occult," or "psychic technology" to get your wishes and desires—to do your will! Quite on the contrary, it is a basic avenue to "let go of your own will and ideas," to tune into, become aware of, and harmonize with God's Will and Mind. Hence, a great deal of prayer is misconceived and misapplied if it is viewed as a way to get Heaven, or the Higher Powers to do your will or to do what you want the most or what you think is the most important for you, or for someone else, at a given point of time.

Prayer, as we saw, is a major way to expand and transform one's consciousness where, indeed, our perceptions, conceptions, priorities, and desires can change dramatically. As the proper position in prayer is always "feminine" vis-a-vis the Superconscious and the Self, the Higher Powers, we have to "empty" and "purify" ourselves of our own human personal thoughts, conceptions, desires, and requests—to better attune to and become receptive of the "higher perspective" brought about by spiritual consciousness. Thus, the first basic step is, indeed, to "let go of our will and perspective," of our conceptions and desires to begin to perceive, feel, and receive what is truly essential from a higher Plane—to become aware of God's Perspective and Will. And, once this is accomplished, then we can invoke and bring through the higher energies and forces, of our being and of the cosmos, to realize and incarnate God's Will—whatever it might be! And this is why the traditional "emotional purification" and "personal detachment" are so important. Thus, before obtaining real "power" and "life" to incarnate our ideas and ideals, we need the realization that we really "know nothing" from the "Higher" or "spiritual" perspective.

Prayer, correctly understood and practiced, can bring about a triple transformation and effect:

a. It will touch and change our psychospiritual Head Center, or mind, expanding our consciousness and bringing more knowledge and understanding about what is truly important and about what is going on.
b. It will touch and change our psychospiritual Heart Center, or emotional core, changing, transforming, and vivifying our feelings and desires. This may express itself in two basic ways: in the awakened desire for a new life, letting go of our old desires and wants, or, in awakening feeling as something genuine and intense where before we felt dullness or emptiness.

c. It will touch and affect our psychospiritual Shoulder Centers or will, vivifying, intensifying, and increasing the life force, creative energies, or the power we have to incarnate and realize God's Will for us. Thus, it can lead us to the realization and direct experience that we are never completely helpless, that we can always "make a difference" and change something.

This triple transformation, or *metanoia*, has the final impact of bringing hope, faith and joy to our entire being as we expand our consciousness, transform our perceptions, conceptions, and desires, and realize what our particular situation is really all about, together with the fact that we can change things and consciously carry out God's Will in this world.

Prayer is also the most important way we find, commune with, and finally unite with our spiritual Self, or Divine Spark. Hence, it is a telepathic means to communicate with our true self and, through the self, with God. As such, it is also one of the most powerful and effective ways of accelerating our evolution and of actualizing our human and spiritual potentials. And, as it is God's Mind and Will that are sought, rather than our own, it is also a very safe, balanced, and effective spiritual exercise. For when we become aware of and commune with the higher energies—the Divine Light, Fire, and Life—our deepest needs and longings are met.

3. What are the most important and practical prayers in our own Christian tradition?

Thomas Keating, a contemporary contemplative monk, gives us an interesting glimpse into the history of prayer in the Christian tradition:

> A positive attitude toward contemplation characterized the first fifteen centuries of the Christian era. Unfortunately, a negative attitude has prevailed from the sixteenth century onward. To understand the situation in which we find our churches today in regard to religious experience, an overview of the history of contemplative prayer may prove helpful.
>
> The word contemplation is an ambiguous term because over the

> centuries it has acquired several different meanings. To emphasize the experiential knowledge of God, the Greek Bible uses *gnosis* to translate the Hebrew *da'ath*, a much stronger term that implies an intimate kind of knowledge involving the whole person.
>
> The Greek Fathers, especially Clement of Alexandria, Origen, and Gregory of Nyssa, borrowed from the Neoplatonists the term *theoria*. This originally meant the intellectual vision of truth, which Greek philosophers regarded as the supreme activity of the person of wisdom. To this technical term the Fathers added the meaning of the Hebrew *da'ath*, that is, the kind of experiential knowledge that comes through love. It was with this expanded understanding of the term that *theoria* was translated into the Latin *contemplatio* and handed down to us in the Christian tradition.
>
> This tradition was summed up by Gregory the Great at the end of the sixth Century when he described contemplation as the knowledge of God that is impregnated with love. For Gregory, contemplation is the fruit of reflection on the word of God in scripture and at the same time a gift of God. In this resting or stillness, the mind and heart are not actively seeking Him but are beginning to experience, to taste, what they have been seeking. This places them in a state of tranquility and profound interior peace. This state is not the suspension of all action, but the mingling of a few simple acts of will to sustain one's attention to God with the loving experience of God's presence.
>
> This meaning of contemplation as the knowledge of God based on the intimate experience of His presence remained the same until the end of the Middle Ages . . . These three acts—discursive meditation, affective prayer, and contemplation—might all take place during the same period of prayer. They are interwoven one into the other. Like the angels ascending and descending on Jacob's Ladder, one's attention was expected to go up and down the ladder of consciousness.[3]

Given that prayer is so important for our well-being, growth, and self-expression, what are the most important prayers I can and should use in my life? Drawing from my own studies and personal experiences, I would begin by saying: *it is not the specific prayer we are saying that is most important, but how we are saying it* that is the crucial element. This means that we could be saying all kinds of prayers from all kinds of traditions—including prayers that we have made up—and obtain no results. As we saw before, prayer is really a function of our level of consciousness, and results depend upon our faith. Nevertheless, we can make a selection of a few basic prayers we are going to live with and make come alive in our consciousness, for to pray we must focus on some specific prayer.

What I have been doing for many years, and with very good results, is saying a combination of traditional prayers drawn from my own religion, and prayers I have made up to suit my own needs and aspirations at the time. While the former remain the same, the latter do change as I change. And, of course, the same could be done with the prayers of any religion. The prayers I use, the ways in which I use them, and the preparation for their use, together with their rationale and explanation have been described at length in my other books.[4] They are:

A. What I have called the "Seven fundamentals" or "basic pillars" of the Western spiritual tradition, namely:

1. The Divine Names or Names of Power (the Names of the Holy Trinity, of our Heavenly Father, of Jesus Christ, of the Blessed Virgin Mary, of the Angels, and of the Saints).
2. The Sign of the Cross.
3. The Lord's Prayer.
4. The Hail Mary.
5. The Nicene Creed.
6. The Beatitudes.
7. The Ten Commandments.

B. Other major Christian Prayers, such as the Trisagion or "Invocation of the Holy Spirit," the Prayer of St. Francis, and Traditional Orthodox Prayers. Of these, the Catholic Mass and the Orthodox Liturgy would be examples of the most complete prayers assembled together to form important spiritual exercises, that is, ways to connect, commune, and unite with the Christ within.

C. The Jesus Prayer, or "Heart Prayer," of the Hesychast tradition: "O Lord Jesus Christ, Son of God, Savior, have mercy upon me a sinner." Or simply: "Lord have Mercy," "Christ have mercy," or "Jesus is my All."

D. A variety of prayers which I have made up for various purposes, and which change from time to time to suit my unfolding consciousness, specific needs, realizations, or aspirations; for example:

O Heavenly Father, Creator and Maker of the Great and Wondrous Universe, the very Source and Essence of all Light, Fire, and Life, have mercy upon me a sinner, grant to fill my spiritual, mental, emotional vital and physical bodies with Thy Light, Fire, and Life so as to heal them, revitalize them, and enable them to carry out the work I am meant to do in this world.

4. What makes prayer become "alive and effective" so that it can bring about immediate transformation in our consciousness?

Let us begin by reemphasizing that prayer is a function of our level of consciousness and being and that it is not the prayer that we say that is the key, but how we say that prayer. The question I am going to try to answer here is how should one pray: what are the psychodynamics involved in prayer as a living channel, one which is capable of working miracles? For it is obvious that in prayer, as in other vital activities, we find many puzzles—one of which (as we mentioned) is that for some prayer remains an empty exercise while for others it becomes the source and channel for bringing through the strongest force in the world. Why this enormous disparity, and what is it that enables one to go from the "letter" to the "spirit" of the prayer?

There are many factors, but an important one is the proper knowledge and correct use of what I call the "muscles of human consciousness." To understand what these are and how they operate we must go back to a basic model of the psyche, or an explanation of human consciousness and how it operates. The most advanced and holistic model of the psyche we have to date is, I believe, that proposed by Psychosynthesis, developed by Roberto Assagioli. The Psychosynthetic model of the psyche is grounded upon the "egg of psychosynthesis" which describes seven structural components located on an egg-like diagram, and upon the "star or flower of psychosynthesis" which shows diagrammatically the seven psychic functions. What I have added to the seven functions of the psyche are the seven psychological processes involving their use, which I have called the "muscles of human consciousness."

The Seven Functions of the Psyche	The Seven "Muscles of Consciousness"
1. Willing	Concentration
2. Thinking	Meditation
3. Emotion	Devotion
4. Intuition	Invocation-Evocation
5. Imagination	Visualization
6. Biopsychic Drive and Impulse	Direction and transformation of biopsychic energies.
7. Sensation	Observation, outer and inner

Of the seven "muscles of consciousness," the specific "muscles" crucial in making prayer come alive are: *concentration, meditation, devotion, visualization, and invocation-evocation.* In simple words, this means that if one cannot concentrate on the given prayer (or on any object for that matter), if one cannot meditate on the given prayer, if one cannot express devotion in that prayer, and if one cannot visualize one or more symbols for that prayer (so that the process of invocation-evocation that activates the intuition will be set in motion), then the prayer will remain sterile, a mere mental or mechanical exercise. Such a prayer is unlikely to contact, activate, and bring through the higher energies. Thus, to pray effectively and in a living way one must first get acquainted with, develop, and coordinate the use of these "muscles." And this normally involves a long and progressive training and mastery.

In the Bible and in Christian tradition, we find many clues and indications to this effect. For example, we are taught to "Love the Lord," our God, with all our Heart (devotion), Mind (meditation), and Soul (concentration), focusing on an image or symbol or event of our choice (visualization). And these four muscles, used together, would then activate and turn on the intuition (invocation-evocation). Another example is when, at Christmas, we are told that The Three Magi, or The Three Wise Kings of the East, came to worship the Christ child, bringing gold, frankincense, and myrrh. The Three Magi can be seen to correspond to concentration, meditation, and devotion, with gold representing human knowledge, myrrh the human will, and frankincense human love;

all of which have to be brought forth as presents or channels for the Divine Light, Fire, and Life. One of the images that can present itself for visualization is then the manger scene with Three Magi bearing their gifts.

Another fundamental element of the prayer is a preliminary exam of consciousness, purification, and consecration of one's consciousness and energies. This can encompass a range of preparations, for example, using the ritual of Confession and Absolution of the Catholic Tradition, special prayers, as well as the "Consciousness Checklist" (see Appendix C). All will facilitate cleaning and activating certain psychospiritual centers as well as our vital, emotional, and mental energy fields or auras.

A final preliminary element to prepare ourselves for living prayer is the systematic reequilibration, relaxation, and stimulation of our vital (or etheric), emotional (or astral), and mental bodies. (This is done either alone or in a group.) The road to living prayer is long and arduous, as is that of any art or discipline which requires the cultivation, development, and coordination of various faculties. In the case of prayer, the specific goal is to make our faith grow; for it is faith that is the key to prayer and that itself rests on the Trinity as this is reflected in the involvement of our minds, hearts, and wills, focused on a basic image, or symbol (which involves the imagination and thus visualization), and that will activate the intuition (invocation-evocation). In simple words, if we want to contact and to bring through the higher energies, we have to bring forward our gifts: our efforts to stir up our will, enabling us to use it; our thinking to stir up our minds; and our feeling to stir up our emotions and love. As a point of focus for all this, we always have a core image or symbol or a series of images and symbols, that involves the use of our imagination. This will activate and awaken our intuition; and it is the intuition that provides the bridge through which the Divine Light, Fire and Life can flow into our consciousness.

As Evelyn Underhill explains it:

> . . . You, accepting the wide deep universe of the mystic, and the responsibilities that go with it, have by this act taken sides once and for all with creative spirit: with the higher tension, the unrelaxed effort,

> the passion for a better, more intense, and more significant life. The adoration to which you are vowed is not an affair of red hassocks and authorized hymnbooks; but a burning and consuming fire . . . If your new life is worth anything, it will flame to sharper power when it strikes against this dogged inertness of things: for you need resistance on which to act. "The road to a Yea lies through a Nay," . . . [5]

5. What is the "essential secret" of prayer?

Prayer involves human effort and divine Grace. In the preceding rubric we have considered human effort—the preparation, the expansion of human consciousness, the focused use of the core "Muscles of Human Consciousness," purification, consecration, and the re-equilibration, relaxation, and stimulation of our three basic "energy bodies" to allow us to be and to express ourselves better. Now we shall focus upon divine Grace, which is the true secret of prayer. Once we have done our part—and we must do our part, for if we bring nothing of ourselves to prayer, we shall receive nothing from prayer—then Divine Grace comes into play; or rather, it is the Self, the Divine Spark, the Christ within us, that must pray rather than the human self. This is the truly arcane or esoteric secret of prayer and the most vital feature, the most powerful energy capable of bringing about miracles.

Here, we may use an interesting image: the words, attention, and efforts (the concentration, meditation, devotion, and visualization) of the human self, from the level of the field of consciousness, are just like a starter of an automobile, but not the motor. The starter is designed to warm up and get the motor started, but it does not do the work of the motor itself and cannot power the automobile. If we insist on using the starter to drive the car instead of the motor, either we shall burn the starter or nothing will happen and the car will not move. The same is true of prayer. True prayer is done and occurs in the Heart Center (as it does at the altar of a church, which represents the Heart Center in the microcosm). It is here in the Heart Center that both the human and the spiritual Self must pray, meet, commune, and unite. It is the human self and the field consciousness that must do the preliminary work, that must act as the trigger for the work of the spiritual Self and of the superconscious.

After we have made the effort of concentration, meditation, devotion, and visualization, and have gone through the necessary preliminaries, all at once we shall feel, see, and experience the Light, Fire, and Life pouring down from on high, from the Head into the Heart Center. The Self, the Christ within, can take over, praying in our consciousness, in our heart. It is then that prayer will truly become alive, for then is it capable of bringing about the threefold internal transformation of our thoughts, feelings, and willing; which, in turn, can bring about transformations of our behavior and of the outside physical world. It is also then that the "Cross of Light" can become activated, vibrating, in our three Energy Bodies, and that we can stand in the presence of God and experience what the Apostle calls "praying without ceasing." This is when we experience prayer uniting all the basic characteristics discussed in the previous rubric. Namely, it makes us aware of God's Mind or Perspective and of God's Will, enabling us consciously to realize them and to incarnate them in our lives, which is the true purpose of prayer. Rather than satisfying our own needs, wishes, and desires, the "will of the ego," this prayer is the embodied affirmation of "Thy Will, not mine, be done." First, though, we must develop and give the very best of ourself—all our attention and energies, all our knowledge and thinking, and all our love and feeling, focused upon a central image or symbol.

Thus, the true spiritual secret of prayer, that which reshapes and remakes us in new life and conforms us to His Omnipotent Will, His Wisdom, His Love is . . . simply to have God pray in us!

6. What preliminary training and discipline can be used to help make prayer become more alive and effective in our own consciousness and life?

There are, of course, various kinds of training and disciplines that can make us become proficient and help us grow in prayer. Some focus primarily upon individual work while others focus on group work, while others yet, on a synthesis of both—which is the approach that I would recommend. For there are certain things that can only be done alone, while others that can only be done in a group. Thus, I would recommend three forms of preliminary training and discipline:

a. Individual prayers along the lines indicated in this chapter (discussed in more depth and detail in *The Nature and Use of Ritual for Spiritual Attainment* and *The Invisible Temple.*)

b. Ritual, especially path-work ritual, as proposed and carried out by a valid Esoteric Order or Temple of the Mysteries.

c. The Roman Catholic Mass, the Orthodox Liturgy, or the High Protestant services, as well as liturgical events as appropriate to the time of year and the liturgical calendar.

The very best combination, in my opinion and practice, is to combine and alternate individual and group prayer with an organic and sequential growth and development. This means to pray alone every day, in the morning, upon waking up, at noon, and in the evening before going to sleep; and perhaps at additional times during the day. These prayers should have both a central and unchanging core and additional prayers that can grow, change, and unfold through time as the consciousness of the individual expands and transforms itself. Then, it can be very useful to have group work. Guidelines for setting up and maintaining such a "Circle of Light" can be found in *The Invisible Temple.* This group work will add immeasurably to the work that is being done alone, just as the work done in solitude will contribute a great deal to the group work. This group work also constitutes an organic growth and development that will train and unfold the psychospiritual sensibilities and capabilities of an individual and will help them to function in a group setting (which has applications both on the visible and invisible sides, on the physical and non-physical planes). This work is also preparatory to full and conscious participation in the Christian Mass, or liturgy, which culminates in the conscious communion with Christ, which is the ultimate spiritual experience towards which all authentic spiritual work aims—but, perhaps, phrasing this aim in different words and ways. (In other traditions, it may be called "union with the self," the "Conversation with one's Holy Guardian Angel," or "establishing a conscious contact with the Divine Spark.")

According to one's training, beliefs, and religious and spiritual associations, one can then follow either the liturgical calendar of one's church, the basic training and program of a spiritual organization, or a self-directed program of spiritual training. All of these can include unfolding and growing prayers. In a self-directed program, a prerequisite is that one has activated one's intuition so that one has an open channel of inspiration to guide this program. For completely alone and left to one's own devices, one could get lost in the "psychic and astral jungles" encountered on the way to the spiritual realms.

In discerning the qualifications of a personal and spiritual growth program two fundamentals are essential: First, that the program and training be authentic and based on a valid outer-and inner-plane tradition, tested by many men and women over a long period of time. Second, that its daily, weekly, monthly, and yearly prayer and exercise program be lived and carried out, putting the utmost of one's self into it—that is, all of one's mind, heart, and will.

The quintessence here, as for other arts and disciplines, is practice, practice, and again, practice—but practice that is consciously done, knowing, at least to some extent, why one is doing something and how to do it most effectively. The greatest esoteric mysteries can only be discovered by living them, by practicing the exercises which can eventually reveal the deepest meanings, implications, and applications. One must trust, too, that, as with all other growth and development in living beings, there is a profound organic sequence of unfolding, which proceeds in its own good time.

7. How to organize one's self and one's life to include a "healthy dose" of prayer?

As prayer and the unfolding of spiritual consciousness are both art and science, there are both valid universal rules and unique applications. Here self-knowledge as well as a deeper understanding of one's life, destiny, and particular conditions are very important. For what may be medicine for one person in one situation may be poison for another person in another situation. Above all, one cannot and should not force anything along spiritual lines. The work must be done. Prayer is to be regularly lived, but one must also wait for the right time to get started and to find the right rhythm and dose.

The fundamental point is to realize the profound nature and the fundamental importance of prayer in his or her life and to make the firm commitment to dedicate systematic and regular attention, time, and energy to a prayer life. Unless this is done, all the rest will be a mere intellectual speculation. In this world, our attention, time, energy, and resources are both precious and limited, so that we have to consciously allocate them according to our values and priorities. Another major point is that it is not the marathon prayer retreat or practice done once in a while under a particular stimulus (of reading a book or attending a workshop) or impetus (an inner drive or curiosity) that can suffice to reach the objectives we have spoken of. Rather, it is regular praying, done even for ten minutes a day, but over a long time, that will make prayer come alive for us. Like all other important aspects of our lives, prayer must become an integral part of our daily lives and being—just like eating, drinking, sleeping, breathing, and interacting with other human beings. Once we have come to that realization and commitment, then it becomes possible to develop a serious and steady program of praying, both alone and in a group. Thus, it is important to plan regular prayer sessions, both individual and group, as well as out of the ordinary ones, reserved for special occasions.

After having studied the nature, functions, purpose, and psychodynamics of prayer, one should then begin to pray regularly every day, setting a minimum of one period to an average of three periods for regular prayer, using the prayers that one has selected and developed for oneself. Then, one could also become involved in regular group work—for example, the "Circle of Light"—and attend Mass, the Liturgy, or other religious services. Finally, one can plan special prayer retreats, pilgrimages to sacred places or shrines, and group rituals for special occasions (for example, the Christian festivals, the equinoxes or solstices, or one's birthday). One can also plan to follow and participate actively in the Catholic or Orthodox liturgical calendar with its special holy days, feasts, and celebrations, or with one of the monastic rules. A study of the Catholic or Orthodox breviary can also provide very rich material and insights.

A final point is to remember to pray whenever one is facing a special crisis, a major decision, or a basic change in one's life. This helps us to obtain greater clarity and insights, to activate intuition, to receive Divine Light and Life, and to obtain blessings. Remember to pray both when things are not going well, when facing a major crisis, but also when things are going very well, to express gratitude and thankfulness. In times of well-being one can open a channel between the field of consciousness and the Superconscious and between the human and the Spiritual Self, which can then be used in all situations.

A very simple example from my own life happened in Italy, at the end of December in 1989. At the time, I was in Milan visiting my mother, giving a lecture/workshop tour and preparing for a possible television interview in Rome—one that could have, it seemed, tremendous implications for both my publishing and lecturing in Italy. As a good Gemini, I tried, once again, to mix heaven and earth, work and fun, inner and outer activities. This time, however, I got caught in the maelstrom of the Italian *dolce vita*—of work, social activities, and festivities. I ate too much, slept too little, and did not protect myself enough from temperature changes, and so I caught a very bad strain of flu. The doctor told me in no uncertain terms that I had two choices, equally unacceptable to me in view of my commitments. These were to stay in bed for a week, or at least until my fever subsided; or to go out and "push" for a day or two and then to go back to bed but, this time, for at least two to three weeks. The verdict seemed inexorable and without appeal.

I was devastated and very angry with myself. I had to give several lectures/workshops in Milan that had been advertised for a long time; I had promised to meet with several people who, I felt, would feel quite hurt if I did not see them; finally, I had to prepare my major TV interview or miss that opportunity. Thus, I was in quite a pickle and in a human, all-too-human (and common) one at that. I immediately thought of prayer—of increasing and intensifying my prayer life. I put it into practice immediately, in spite of my aches, fatigue, and lack of concentration. Prayer had helped so many times, in so many ways, that surely it would help me again—if only in understanding and accepting my situation. As I prayed, putting all my heart and devotion into the process, I soon understood quite clearly that I had abused myself, violated several laws, lowered my resistance and my immune system. The next step was even more dismal; with a strange sense of humor my higher Self seemed to tell me that I, of all people, should know (as that is what I preached and wrote) that prayer was not a way to obtain what "I" (my lower self) wanted, that it was not a magical tool, or a psychospiritual technique to abrogate natural law or to avoid the unpleasant consequences that I had set in motion by my own attitudes and actions. Rather, it is a way to achieve a conversion, a true metanoia, where one's way of thinking, feeling, and willing change dramatically. It is a way to expand one's consciousness to connect with the consciousness and will of the higher Self, and ultimately of God. Duly chastened, I was then ready to learn my lesson, which I would never forget. I would never push and abuse myself as I had done, especially when I had so many more important things to do. I had to learn patience and acceptance of the situation, and do the best I could staying in bed, maybe fasting a little and praying more.

At the end of that session, however, when I had fully but sorrowfully accepted my situation, an image suddenly appeared with an impulse and the energy to act on it. I saw the image of a healing Madonna in a little sanctuary, where I would occasionally go to pray and which was renowned for its healing properties, just three minutes' walk from my mother's apartment. I decided that there was no time like now and that since I would have to stay in bed for a week anyway, I might as well get up and go pray in front of that icon. So I put my clothes on and went to the sanctuary and prayed with all the concentration, meditation, and devotion I could muster. Very soon I felt my consciousness expanding, my vibrations rising, and something like a cool breeze or current flow through my head right straight to my feet, little by little filling my whole being and consciousness. I could feel my Head, Heart, Feet, and Shoulder Centers, as well as my Hip and Yesod or Sexual Center, really come alive and begin to pulsate or vibrate. At that point, I forgot myself and everything else and just basked in that wonderful energy and the feelings evoked. Tears ran down my cheeks and I felt an intense heat in my Heart Center and then a coolness rise from my feet to spread to my whole being. I also felt as though I had lost a great deal of weight as well as all my worries, hurry, and other concerns. I felt an incredible joy envelop my consciousness, and wonderful gratitude.

After a while I got up and went back home, feeling very different, transformed. I still felt somewhat weak and disoriented, but I took my temperature and noticed that the fever was gone. As it was already evening, I turned off the light and fell asleep. When I woke up the next morning, I knew that I was healed, and got up and picked up where I had left off, not missing one lecture, workshop, or meeting, and being able to accomplish all I had set out to do—and more, for I had learned a very important lesson, or should I say lessons. I concluded that I should be more prudent in the future, that I should pray more and seek to keep in conscious contact with the Will of the Lord Who, obviously, this time, had allowed me to do what I was meant to do, in spite of my own foolishness and weaknesses. I ended up doing everything I had planned with much more joy, gratitude, and appreciation for what I was doing than I would have done otherwise. I learned that we can benefit and be enriched even from our mistakes if God's Light is kept present and flowing in our consciousness and being. This is what the living and practical part of esoteric Christianity is all about.

In conclusion, let me say that prayer involves not only feeding our Soul, expanding our state of consciousness, raising our vibrations and life-force, and activating and lighting up our Tree of Life with its psychospiritual Centers and our Auras (energy bodies): it includes also a "male" and a "female" polarity. The "female" aspect consists in activating and opening up our sensitivity and receptivity on the four fundamental planes of our being—the physical, emotional, mental, and spiritual—so that we can be open and sensitive to what comes from above, from the spiritual dimension. It consists, essentially, in letting go of our egoistic will, thoughts, and striving. The "male" polarity consists in intensifying and vivifying our vital energies and in increasing our life force. This implies the very opposite of the "female" polarity—making the maximum effort of concentration, meditation, devotion, and visualization. This can be a paradox, as we see in the development and the surrender of our will and ego: With effort we develop both and raise them to their highest level of functioning in order to offer them to the Divine once they are developed and functioning. Yet this is truly one of the most difficult things to do, for those who are best at making efforts are usually the worst at letting go and vice versa. Moreover, if one has spent a great deal of time and energy and made great efforts and sacrifices to develop something (the will, the ego, or other abilities), one finds it very difficult, if not contradictory, to let it go and sacrifice it, to "give it up" as it were. And yet, this is precisely what the authentic art of prayer and the genuine spiritual life demand of us.

It is also helpful to keep a prayer diary with accurate and regular entries of what we have done, when, in what fashion, and with what immediate and (or delayed) results. And it can be of great help to share one's experiences with other brothers and sisters on the Path and to have the advice and guidance of a teacher or a spiritual director. This is true for any art, discipline, or practice, and it is particularly true of the life of prayer, which is full of the unexpected.

If one wants to become a fully actualized and realized human being, the art and science of prayer is indispensable and fulfills a role that cannot be fulfilled by anything else. The more we evolve our consciousness, the more important spiritual "nourishment" becomes. One could almost say that, from a certain point onwards, it becomes more important for one's well-being and proper functioning to pray than it is to eat food or interact with other human beings. But this is something to discover through your own personal experience. Try not to eat and drink for a few days and see what happens to your body and psyche. Once prayer has become alive in you, it will create the same hunger and thirst but on a different level of your consciousness and being. At that point, you will also discover what Evelyn Underhill has so aptly described.

"Because of your new sensitiveness, anthems will be heard of you from every gutter; poems of intolerable loveliness will bud for you on every weed. Best and greatest, your fellow-men will shine with new significance and light. Humility and awe will be evoked in you by the beautiful patient figures of the poor, their long dumb heroism, their willing acceptance of the burden of life."[6]

SAINT-JACQUES
en pélerin
Bourgogne, XVe siècle

CHAPTER FIVE

Pilgrimage: The Inner and Outer Journey to the Holy Place

What is life on earth, if not a great adventure? The literature of centuries abounds in myths, legends, and tales of the Quest as the central metaphor of life with its series of adventures and misadventures, of trials, joys, and sufferings that are lived and recorded, sometimes as tragedies, sometimes as comedies. Of all human adventures, the spiritual Quest is unquestionably the greatest, speaking across all recorded history of an ancient longing—at least, if we are to judge from that oldest of human myths, the epic of Gilgamesh, where what motivates a king to leave his kingdom and all he loves is the search for everlasting life. Still and ever, it is that most alluring of beckonings, the call to the essential adventure that takes us to the heart of life, and of who we are.

The pilgrimage has always played a central role in all authentic philosophical systems, religions, and spiritual traditions. It generally means a journey in the world towards a Sacred Place, a Sanctuary, a Cathedral, or shrine, together with a special preparation and specific spiritual exercises to carry out. It is a microcosm of our life on earth, with its terrors, anxieties, desires, aspirations, and unforecasted events, and we bring what we have learned of life along with us on this journey, for better or for worse.

In the interior of cathedrals that have served as the culminating points of pilgrimages, one can often find a labyrinth located in the central aisle. This labyrinth represents the journey inside one's self that corresponds, homologically, to the pilgrimage in the external world. Thus in all external pilgrimages in the world, we find the reflection of the inner journey to the core of our being. Here, the fundamental objective is not to get to the holy place as fast as possible, but is to be found within the trip itself, with all of its changing scenery, misadventures, efforts, external and internal discoveries, encounters and surprises. The central destination of the inner and outer pilgrimage, towards a holy place, a sanctuary, to the center of the labyrinth, is always the same: it is the inner Christ and the celestial Jerusalem, our true country or home.

All the great spiritual traditions and religions have described and recommended pilgrimages to one or more Sanctuaries or Holy Places at a certain time of the year. This is so of the three great religions of the West—Judaism, Christianity, and Islam; as well as in the four religions of the East—Hinduism, Buddhism, Taoism, and Shintoism. To mention only a few of the best known pilgrimages, we have those to cathedrals and sanctuaries of Lourdes, Chartres, Paris, and Rheims in France; The Oratory of Saint Joseph, the Sanctuary of the Cap de la Madeleine, and St. Anne de Beaupres in Quebec, Canada; Santiago de Compostela in Spain; Medjugorje in Yugoslavia; Mecca in Saudi Arabia for the Muslim; the Western Wall in Jerusalem for the Jew. Almost every country, as every religion, has its own high or holy places for pilgrimages.

To truly live a pilgrimage, one needs to know and be able to use the three basic functions of human consciousness—that is, willing (through the effort that is required), thinking (through the planning and reflections that are required), and feeling (through the love and desire that motivate this experience). From the esoteric viewpoint, it is movement, effort, and activity that activate our will, our vital force and creative energies that make Life flow through us. Likewise, it is thinking, meditation, and reflection that set in motion **consciousness** and understanding—which make Light flow through us. Finally, it is feeling, profound emotions, and passion that awaken and activate Love in us, that make Fire flow through us. This is the reason why all authentic pilgrimages must absolutely be difficult, cost us efforts, and shake us up so as to make us come out of our usual lethargy. They must also make us think, direct all our attention and thoughts on its nature and its objective, knowing we are bound to encounter paradox and the mysterious. Above all, the pilgrimage must shake us up emotionally and make us feel deeply this triple impact upon our consciousness, experienced through all the symbols, images, colors, sounds, and objects, and the vicissitudes we have to undergo to arrive at the Holy Place.

Pilgrimages also entail two basic dimensions: the objective dimension (the sanctuary, the churches, the road, the difficulties to get to these holy places, the preparation, the services and rituals one goes through). And the subjective dimension (the state of being, the attitude, the level of consciousness, as well as the energies and functions of the psyche which are involved and used). The basic aim of a pilgrimage is to get out of the routine and torpor of everyday life in which we are only half-conscious, half-awakened, and half-alive, to shake us up and free our latent energies and lights. And it is especially through a sustained effort and a deep and intense emotion and focused devotion that we can achieve this.

There are one or more holy places having sanctuaries where there are fountains; this water can be charged with etheric energies and suffused with the telluric currents coming from a mountain or a special place. There are also holy places where the relics of a saint are kept, another possible place where miraculous healings occur. There are often statues, frescoes, or paintings commemorating heroic or sacred deeds that have occurred in this place; we can encounter images and symbols, services and rituals, all of which affect our senses—our seeing, hearing, smell and touch—to reinforce and concentrate our will, thoughts, emotions, imagination, and intuition. We bring ourselves to the holy place so that after the considerable effort and the physical and psychological tension to get there, we can have a letting go, a relaxation, and the culminating moment—both sides of the great alternation between the masculine and feminine polarities, between human effort and the descent of grace.

Interiorly, one must go through a progressive and organic preparation dealing with emptying and filling our being and consciousness. This is what is generally known as fasting and praying but it can be done on several levels—the physical, emotional, mental, and spiritual level. It is this preparation with fasting and praying that leads to a conversion or *metanoia*—a transformation of our thoughts, emotions, willing, imagination, and intuition. Here we see again the three stages of purification, consecration, and union with the Superconscious and the self (the Divine Spark). These, in turn, will affect and transform the seven functions as well as the structural components of our psyche (the field of consciousness, the preconscious, subconscious, unconscious, and superconscious).

No true pilgrim remains passive and a mere spectator. She or he must get involved with his or her whole being in this process. The results and the experiences we can hope to have are directly related to, though not totally determined by, this involvement and conscious participation: one cannot approach the sacred greedily for what one wants to achieve, even if what one wants is spiritual consciousness. One gives of oneself freely and humbly to the Higher Powers within and without us without thought or expectation of what can or should be given to us in return. Yet we can hope to be worthy—indeed, all our preparation is for this. We can bring our best efforts, our attention, our creative energies, thoughts and reflections, emotions and feelings, all into accord as an offering. And we can have hope and faith that truly seeking, we shall find; knocking, the door will be opened. The more we can offer of ourselves, the more can the spiritual energies, prismated into and apprehended as Divine Light, Fire, and Life, manifest and transform our consciousness and being. This is also why a pilgrimage is a personal and subjective experience even though it is often lived in a community or collective setting, that of the church, for example, and with fellow-pilgrims.

Let us go to the culminating moment during which the pilgrim finds himself in the sanctuary, the crypt, the place of the miraculous, of apparitions and of healing. A human being can become, in that moment of epiphany, of joyous *episteme*, after the long arduous journey, now centered within and moving through his or her Tree of Life (as we have seen, the psychospiritual Centers and the Energy Bodies, the auras), a filament, heated white hot and illuminated. How this occurs involves the current of life and energy that can flow from the Astral World to the Etheric World and, in a place of pilgrimage where water is a central element, by the action of water and earth through an angelic impulsion and inspiration. This creates an atmosphere through which the higher spiritual energies can manifest, refining our consciousness, invigorating us, giving us the sense of *joie de vivre* in a more amplified and dynamized way.

A pilgrimage can, therefore, be lived as a peak-experience, as an experience of the heights, which stands outside everyday life and the ordinary as a kind of psychological and spiritual mountain-climbing. On the "Holy Mountain" dwell the spiritual beings who can reach out and help us, the celestial hierarchies of angels, the saints and sages in the spiritual world, but most of all, Christ, both as Son of God and as the Divine Spark within, the spiritual Self. If gifts are given, the blessing of visions, understanding, intuitions, the re-equilibration of being, the reframing of judgment, of discernment, of proportions, these are not ends in themselves but enable us to integrate all of this, to manifest in it in daily life. It is this that must be transformed by the pilgrimage experience, for it is indeed daily life, with all of its experiences, adventures, and tests, with their success or failure, that constitutes the true "earthly school," the "laboratory" of our becoming, and the actualization of our faculties and potential. Pilgrimages must, therefore, have a profound impact and repercussions on our daily life and should ideally, be undertaken at regular periods in our lives to provide alternation between the ascensions to the peaks of our consciousness and the normal walks in the valleys.

Nor does a pilgrimage always present itself as one explicitly, but later, in retrospect, we can realize that in taking up a new venture we did truly enter into a life-changing pilgrimage, for what was found there was as described above. Let me give an example from my own life.

As a student in primary and secondary schools, I was doing very badly. Unmotivated, not respecting my teachers. I, in my wisdom, did not feel I could learn anything meaningful and practical for life and so spent most of my time making mischief and making my schoolmates laugh. I had made mine, Molière's proverb, "rire et faire rire" (to laugh and make others laugh), but at the cost of flunking many subjects or barely passing the year. As I left for the United States, at the age of seventeen, I had a very low high school grade average and was, for all practical purposes, a high school drop out. I am not the only one who was ever in that unfortunate situation, but perhaps I am one of the few who was later to go on to receive several graduate and postgraduate degrees and become a university professor. What brought about this transformation and what spiritual principle was involved in this?

I never graduated from high school and thus, technically, remained a high school drop out. But something happened along the way that radically changed both my outlook and my life. When I was eighteen and had not yet been a year in the United States, I fell very much in love with a girl. Her father eventually told me that, before we could get engaged and plan a life together, I had to make something of myself, complete my education, and find a meaningful occupation of some sort. At that point, I did become motivated to study. I chose an American university in the West that was less strict on admissions credentials and that had a first-class ski team. I managed to convince the admissions committee to give me a chance to prove myself and to give me a skiing scholarship (the one thing I could do well was skiing, having been born in Switzerland and practically on skis).

It was there, in Colorado, that I had an appointment with destiny that was to dramatically change the course of my life. This appointment with destiny was simply meeting a man, George Gamov, a Russian-American astrophysicist who was also a Nobel Laureate. In addition to being a great scientist, he was also a mystic who had achieved a true level of spiritual consciousness—and he spoke French. We became friends and he became my first model of the professors I would later emulate. What he conveyed to me was a vision of the world I could resonate with, a direct understanding of several of my inner experiences, and a great love for learning, as well as a passion for living. In a word, he brought "enthusiasm" to me, in its original Greek meaning of "awakening God within." He also convinced me to transfer to a first class university and to study nuclear physics! And he helped me get into Columbia University, where I went the following year.

Each person has a destiny in this world and when the right time arrives this destiny will be made manifest. Also, there are spiritual powers that watch over us and arrange encounters, situations, and experiences—including pilgrimages—in the right way and at the right moment. Thus, to be true to one's self and one's destiny is most important; then to work, patiently, upon oneself so as to know and perfect oneself in such a way that when the right moment and opportunities do present themselves one can recognize them and make the best of them. There are invisible worlds as well as invisible beings and it is in the invisible worlds that the true causes originate. We are never left alone or truly abandoned. There are spiritual beings that watch over us and that work with us to help our own evolution and becoming, helping us to overcome our weaknesses and to develop and use our qualities. Thus one should never lose hope in the future, reject what life brings us, and give way to frustration and self-pity, for, when all seems to be lost or hopeless, just around the corner may lie the greatest discovery or encounter that which will finally make manifest to us the purpose of this life—what we have come in this world to accomplish and the means to do it.

Daily life—with our work, human relations, problems, fears, and anxieties as well as our desires and aspirations and our successes and failures, and with all the tensions, frustrations, delusions, and hopes they entail—can lead to stress, fatigue, and disequilibrium, which tend to make us strangers to ourselves and strangers to God. For many people, even the strongest, the most courageous, and the most equilibrated, prayer no longer means anything truly vital, alive, or meaningful, and remains perhaps only a felt religious duty. Meditation and relaxation are used, most of the time, for the utilitarian goals of survival, for success in the world, for self-seeking spiritual powers and aims. Work is perceived and defined as a constraint and a duty that life, society, and our family imposes on us, in which one must continually struggle for economic and professional survival. Recreation, fun, leisure have become only a way to "unwind," to drown one's sorrows, unhappiness, and the fatigue of daily routine. Thus, periodically, we have a deep and genuine need to climb the Holy Mountain, to reestablish a conscious contact with the Lord—both within us and as the Other—to receive His Light, Fire, and Life which will enable us to live our daily lives in a more meaningful and productive way.

Another and much better way to renew daily life, one long recognized and practiced by the sacred traditions, is to go on a pilgrimage, from which one returns transformed, regenerated, with new understanding, vitality, and enthusiasm for, precisely, daily life. It can signify and actualize the end of a cycle, of the year, of a way of life, to thus begin a new cycle, a new life. In this way, it is a form of death and resurrection that is enacted and brought about, for we do not need to die physically to start again and begin a new life. One of the fundamental remedies that spiritual tradition proposes is that of organizing our vacations, our "re-creation," as a pilgrimage to a Holy Place. The modern leisure trip or vacation voyage is only a fragment of the earlier and more complete pilgrimage—its secular, physical and emotional counterpart, stripped of spiritual implications and aspects.

To pass now to practice, I would like briefly to describe a pilgrimage that I made not too long ago, during August 1988, when I went to the Oratory of St. Joseph in Montreal and to the Sanctuary of St. Anne de Beaupres, going through the Sanctuary of the Cap de la Madeleine in Quebec, Canada. I dedicated a week to this pilgrimage, seven consecutive days with two actual days of traveling.

The Oratory of St. Joseph, in Montreal, is located on a mountain, Mount Royal, and to reach the Oratory one must go by foot up the mountain (some pilgrims walk the last three hundred feet on their knees). To get to the water fountain of the Oratory one must climb still many more steps. There, almost at the top of the cathedral, one can drink the water imbued with the telluric and cosmic forces of this sanctuary, which act directly on the etheric or vital body to vivify consciousness with their vital energies. I began with a fast, eating only fruit and vegetables; also, I drank a great deal of the water from the Oratory. For four days I prayed, meditated, and did physical and spiritual exercises. I also went every day to visit the tomb of Brother Andre, in the Crypt of the Oratory, and to Mass and Communion as the culminating point. I did this to give praise and thanksgiving, experiencing the Mass in all the ways described earlier in this book, filling my inner Tree of Life, its psychospiritual Centers, and my energy bodies and auras with spiritual energies (Divine Light, Fire, and Life). I also meditated on the life, the teachings, and the healings of Brother Andre as well as on the symbols of the Oratory. After this, I descended into the Crypt to put both my hands, and then also my forehead, on the black marble tomb of Brother Andre, located in the heart of the Crypt. It is a place suffused with very powerful energies and vibrations, condensed and focalized by the many pilgrims who visit it and by the very strong angelic presences.

I prayed and meditated there for a long time. I began feeling my etheric, astral, and mental bodies profoundly touched, then transformed and purified. Thus, in turn, I experienced a consecration of my state of being, at times sending me into "another world." In this state of consciousness, I went to Mass, in the chapel of the Crypt, which, being celebrated here, was quite intense. Also, by repeating this process several times, over several days, the reverberation becomes progressive and cumulative. How to describe this culmination? My entire being, all of my Centers and cells, body and consciousness, began to vibrate and pulsate in such a way that my thoughts, feelings, will, imagination, intuition, and even sensations were deeply changed. One becomes—though this must be experienced to be understood—a new person living in a new world!

On the fifth day, I left for the sanctuary of the Cap de la Madeleine, which is located about seventy miles north of Montreal. Having arrived at the sanctuary, I walked for a certain period of time before entering the chapel to get in touch with the surrounding energies. Entering the sanctuary, I prayed with great fervor and meditated in a focused way, reflecting upon and consciously assimilating the energies and vibrations of this Holy Place. After this, I left again, this time for St. Anne de Beaupres which is located about 240 miles north of Montreal.

Arriving at St. Anne de Beaupres, I looked for a motel to spend the night and, that done, went to the cathedral. With the connection I felt there, there also came the experience of an incredible heat, an indescribable sense of beatitude flowed out of my Heart Center, and tears from my eyes. Again, I felt projected into a new state of consciousness and into another world, alive, vivified, and filled with blessings, with all kinds of discoveries; my consciousness became transparent to my mind, as did the central symbol of these three sanctuaries and its essential objective: the purification, consecration, and perfecting of the four energy bodies of human nature.

I began to understand that these great cathedrals with their sanctuaries, fountains of energized water, and their histories, are enormous accumulators and transformers of Divine Light and Energy, awaiting discovery by those who are ready. I also felt that discovery of these sanctuaries could help enable Quebec and Canada to fulfill their function in the great family of nations of our planet.

The next day, I returned to the cathedral to drink the water from the special fountain, meditate, pray, and attend the Mass and partake of Communion. Having done this, I returned to Montreal. And the next day, the seventh day, I returned to St. Joseph's Oratory to complete my little pilgrimage with the original process, but now lived in a new way. I emerged from this pilgrimage a new being with a new conscience and ready to pick up my normal life again, which then became a new life filled with joy, with strength, with the desire to do things, to do great things in this world!

Louis Charpentier, in his superb work, *The Mysteries of the Cathedral of Chartres,* gives us excellent ideas and practical advice concerning the nature, the internal dynamics, and the essential objectives of the great cathedrals and of pilgrimages. For him a cathedral is an initiatory instrument, and pilgrimages a journey, a path to the center of our own being:

> For the ancients, man was truly human only when his spiritual faculties were awakened. One could reach this either by being born with it or by special training and self-conditioning. A central place was always reserved for this awakening by coming to "holy places" that were the objective of a pilgrimage. All religions, ancient and modern, always had their "High Places" of pilgrimage—the ancient and the modern being, generally, the same.
>
> More sensitive than we are to the action and virtues of natural forces, the ancients knew far better than we do these places. To find them, we must look for the traces they have left behind: megaliths, dolmens, or temples, and such a place is, indeed, Chartres.[1]

Where do these currents of subtle energies capable of affecting human consciousness and human behavior come from? In my opinion, they come from three sources: first, there are the telluric and cosmic currents—from the earth, from the water, from the air, and from the sun; second, there are psychospiritual currents and energies—from human beings; third, there are spiritual currents and energies—for example, from the angelic world. The source as well as the nature of these currents is, therefore, triple—as are all manifestations of Creation. They always flow, or manifest in their masculine-feminine polarity, for life, or power to manifest in reality needs this polarity and essential tension. Charpentier gives some very useful indications:

> Some telluric currents originate in underground water, others from cracks in the rock-layers which connects different strata with different temperatures; others yet from the magma at the core of the earth . . . these currents are the manifestation of the life of the earth. Where they are absent, the earth is dead, unfertile, just like would be a part of the human body which is no longer irrigated by the blood flow. Where these telluric currents manifest, they bring life which makes the earth fertile.[2]

Further on, he continues, giving us specific indications on the nature and function of "stones" as "channels" and "transformers" of these energies:

> Stones possess two remarkable qualities: First, like its little "artificial sister," the brick, a stone is an "accumulator", it "charges" itself with the telluric or cosmic influences. Second, it is made of a substance that can vibrate . . . Stones, therefore, are both accumulators and amplifiers of vibrations.[3]

And he says:

> But this vital current—the Spiritus Mundi of the Alchemists, the Spirit of the World (the Chinese "Earth Dragon")—works ceaselessly on all things, the evolution of which it accelerates, including man. Let us assume that, in certain places because of a special concentration of the "current," this evolutionary force is intensified, all the more so when people are receptive to it. By going to these places, one can go through a natural "mutation," to use a modern term. This is what pilgrimages aim at, working through a kind of "natural alchemy."
>
> Here man becomes, somehow, the "chalice," the "Grail" which captures this energy. He has three basic "paths" to achieve this "mutation," which are represented by three tables: the round table, the square table, and the rectangular table—symbolizing Intuition, Intelligence, and Mysticism.[4]

Connecting all of this to the "Holy Place" of the pilgrimage, to the cathedral, to the temple and its sanctuary, Charpentier concludes:

> The cathedral goes further. It rises in the air. It plunges—and this is why it is built so high—into the aerial currents, the rains of the sky, and the storms of the atmosphere, in the great cosmic currents. It gathers light, it absorbs it, and transforms it . . . It connects earth, water, air, and fire! What was ever more complete to realize the most beautiful human alchemy! Here we are indeed dealing with alchemy and transmutation, not the transmutation of metals but of man, of men that must reach a superior level of humanity. But, to be efficacious, the "instrument" had to be adapted to the Earth, to the Sky, and to Man. One must never forget that cathedrals are built for men, to act upon men, and everything in it was designed with this end in view—that it is, as St. Bernard said, a means.[5]

> The master builder was not doing "art," he was making a cathedral. He sought—and succeeded—in building an instrument for religious action; an instrument which possessed a power over men . . . the power to mutate men . . .
>
> It is an instrument to pass from one world to another; a "bridge" between two worlds . . .
>
> While the pilgrim was in the cathedral, he was bathed and suffused with telluric, visual, and sound energies and vibrations in the midst of which the magical effects of ritual—for rites and ceremonies are magic—took on an extraordinary power and amplitude, which had a deep impact upon the pilgrim.[6]

Finally, he concludes by saying:

> Is it only when man has abandoned all ties with matter that he can obtain the "key" to grasp the complexity of the universe in its totality? Where he can see God, according to the traditional expression, "face to face" . . . The universe embodied in an atom as the atom is embodied in the universe. To lead man to the point, if not of comprehension, at least of "communion" with the world—this is the meaning and purpose of the cathedral, and why I spoke of a utilitarian monument.
>
> The great conquest of Christianity, perhaps the greatest, has been to put at the disposal of all the initiatory monument once reserved to the few privileged who, alone, had access to the interior of the Temples.[7]

The fundamental aim of pilgrimages is thus a practical and an initiatory one. And the initiatory aim is none other than this: to raise the vibrations of human beings, to increase their vital force, to make them more alive in order to transform consciousness.

Speaking of initiation, Charpentier tells us that:

> Initiation was not a "state of knowing," but a "state of being." It is what the early Christians called a "state of grace" (until this term lost its inner, spiritual meaning). One can be in a state of grace and completely ignore the metric system; be in a state of grace and not know anything about theology; . . .
>
> To be initiated is to be introduced; to be reintegrated in the play of cosmic forces, to know them, to incorporate them—etymology speaks very clearly—to feel them in one self, as a superior instinct over which the brain has no control . . . It is to be reconnected with these forces; hence, it is to be religious in the Latin sense of the term ("religare," to bind back or reconnect). In a word, it is to be penetrated and suffused with the Spirit.[8]

Charpentier also gives us a profound, esoteric comprehension of the etymology of the word *gothic* and of the aim of the authentic tradition. Thus he writes:

> The word "gothic" from the Greek *goetie*=magic; *goes*=magician; *goetis*=sorcery; and *goeteou*=to fascinate—designates the art of "casting spells"—the term is quite direct. The romanesque style has this force from above below . . . [the gothic style] has its forces directed from below upwards . . .
>
> The Tables of the Law (by which one builds the great cathedrals) are written on "two sides." This can mean legible upside or upside down; or in two ways, exoterically and esoterically. In today's language, we can say that the Tables of the Law are the Tables of the equation of the universe. Thus to possess the Tables of the Law is to have the possibility to know the great Law of Unity which governs the universe, to go from the effects to the causes and, therefore, to act on the phenomena engendered by the causes as they work towards plurality.
>
> Now you can understand why we spoke of the cathedral as an instrument of action upon man, in the sense of a direct initiation . . . What is truly at stake is human growth and perfection and this growth and perfection would remain incomplete without the existence of initiatory Temples acting directly upon the individual, to awaken in him spirituality without which he would never be complete. [The Master builders] could not avoid the construction of a Temple in such a special place as Chartres where Mother Earth offers her ineffable gift.[9]

And he concludes his analysis by stating that:

> Traditional science is a science in every sense of the term; it is a more complete science than the present one which, through microscope or telescope, sees the universe only externally, as it does not possess the *intus lectio,* the ability to "read from within" (which is the etymology of the word intelligence and intellect). And it is because it was a science engendering "power" that it has been kept hidden, secret, occult . . .
>
> Science is one. Legends sacred writings, carved stones, monuments have a common base which one can find in all initiatory monuments . . . No wonder that these monuments are located in places where the telluric currents can help men to unfold "intelligence," the *intus ligere,* to be able to "read Nature from within" as visible symbol of the Great Law . . .
>
> Everything happened as if, once the initiatory monument completed, men were given back their full free will, just like students once the course is completed. So that they will live their lives as they wish . . . at their risk and peril . . . [10]

To truly grasp and understand the true nature, the psychospiritual dynamics, and the meaning and purpose of a pilgrimage, there is only one way—one must experience it personally, do it, and live it. The present chapter is but a lighthouse and an encouragement to lead you to this great traditional means of initiation and expansion of your consciousness. The rest is up to you.

CHAPTER SIX

Health, Disease, Sin, and Salvation in the Coming Age

The first serious and genuine step towards spirituality involves healing—seeking our holistic health—as the early Christians knew and as all candidates to spiritual initiation well know. "Health" is inner harmony or ease with the laws of nature and of God, just as disease is disharmony, or "lack of ease." But true health is much more than "*mens sana in corpore sano,*" a healthy mind in a healthy body, just as disease is much more than pain and dysfunction in various physical organs or in our psyche. As Dion Fortune rightly points out:

> All seeking should be spiritual healing, even if its outward form be that of a surgical operation. Every curative process, whether applied to the body in a hospital or in the soul in a prison, should be inspired by a spiritual ideal . . . The curative art means readjustment. There is but one absolute standard by which anything can be readjusted, and that is natural law, or the nature of God. All healing, therefore, whether of mind, body, or estate, must aim at bringing that which is amiss into harmony with God's law, that is to say, God's nature as shown us by His Son.
>
> The Great Physician is the Master of all who would make straight that which is crooked, provided they do it for the glory of God and the service of man, and not for their own aggrandisement. His spirit it is which should illuminate all healing work and over shadow every hospital and prison, for in His spirit alone can they fulfill their mission.[1]

A great "paradigm shift," or transformation, is taking place in medicine and in our conception of health, illness, and therapy.

Thus far, we have taken a "Piscean" or dualistic view of health and disease: health is good and illness is bad, just as pleasure is good and suffering bad. And yet each has a place, a function, and a meaning that are ultimately for our own good and evolution.

The first, and perhaps greatest breakthrough and new discovery of this new state of consciousness or paradigm shift is that disease, like suffering, has two faces: both a constructive and a destructive, a positive and a negative face. Thus, we can experience illness as something positive, as an opportunity to grow, to learn, and to improve something. We can come to accept and live illness as a friend, as part of the initiatory way—bringing to us an important message that we must change something in our lives, that we cannot go on the way we are going. Sickness, in other words, can function as an alarm system, requiring attention and action, as well as being a form of invitation to move on to a higher level.

Today, the medical profession, like the clergy, are going through a major crisis, a true re-definition of identity and distinctive function. If there are laws that govern the nature and dynamics of human consciousness, then these are bound to affect the basic rules of human health and the prevention and treatment of human illnesses.

Until recently, the official "allopathic" medicine of the West has been scientific but more in the sense of materialistic and rationalistic rather than truly empirical, i.e., based upon direct observation and personal experience. It has been analytical (as seen in increased specialization) and has focused on the therapeutic, in removing problems once they have occurred. It has focused on alleviating or removing symptoms rather than in exploring and changing the causes. Collectively, it has not open-mindedly regarded "alternative" or "traditional" forms of medicine. It has encouraged reliance on authority and passivity, having the patient "take the pills," unquestioningly undergo surgery or follow a given therapy. It has not encouraged self-reliance, having the person examine and change his or her dysfunctional attitudes, lifestyle, or relationships. And it has been fundamentally a medicine of the physical body.

The new, emerging medical paradigm is very different. It is *scientific* in the sense of taking observation and experience as its final court of appeal; *holistic* in terms of looking at the whole person within the context of his entire life; *preventive* in educating people to understand the laws of life and health rather than curing pathologies; *inclusive* insofar as working together with many different but complementary approaches. Importantly, it focuses at getting to the level of causes rather than remaining content with the alleviation or suppression of symptoms. It does encourage the person to take an active role in examining his or her life, to change dysfunctional attitudes, behaviors, and relationships or to undergo a "reframing" which can deal with the true causes of the problem. And it is becoming more and more a spiritualized medicine, one which takes into account the fact that the human being is more than chemistry and physical matter; it sees the human being as first and foremost a spiritual being, not in any vague sense, but in having higher energy bodies which follow laws and which affect and interact with the physical body.

An early major qualitative step was taken with the so-called "psychosomatic" medicine which saw and dealt with a close connection and interrelationship between the body and the psyche, where negative thoughts, feelings, and energies were seen to create psychological and physical illnesses. Now the question arises, coming full circle in this inquiry, what human illness does *not* have a psychosomatic causative factor, or how can we ask the right spiritual questions to reveal cause and effect patterns in health and disease?

Another line of insight comes from acknowledging the effect of the repression of the sublime, namely, that if a person does not resolve the problems of identity, the "enigma of the Sphinx," and rejects his or her higher energies and inspirations, they fall sick and lose their ease. If people do not know who they fundamentally are, if they do not do what they have in this world to do—if they repress the "voice of their soul," of their divine Spark, they lose harmony and become a cacophony of symptoms. Yet the soul in this way does create a certain pressure, in withdrawing or increasing energies, creating enough discomfort and tension so that the person will pay attention and, it is hoped, change direction and take a new course of action.

While Freud saw religion as an infantile neurosis to be outgrown, Jung saw it as an indispensable element for growth, health, and individuation. Thus have two streams developed in twentieth century medicine; one taking a narrow and basically materialist view of the human being, and the other, becoming more and more prominent now, with a far more multidimensional view. Such a multidimensional view can include levels or the different planes of consciousness. Once the reality of these is experienced, an entirely new set of questions arises concerned with the connection and flow between the various planes, e.g., from the spiritual to the mental, from the mental to the astral, from the astral to the etheric, and from the etheric to the physical plane—and vice versa.

In regards to health and illness, my position is that the proper and healthy function of any of the higher vehicles has a positive and a causal effect on the workings of the lower ones, but not vice versa. That is, a healthy spiritual body, filled with life and harmony, can heal the mental, astral, etheric, and physical body (if the connections are made and the channels are open), but a healthy and vital physical body cannot heal and realign the etheric, astral, mental, and spiritual bodies.

Once the nature and functioning of the energy bodies are understood and experienced, then will many of the "new" alternative therapies (which in fact are often quite old) such as homeopathy, acupuncture, and the laying-on-of-hands begin to make sense; so also will prayer, ritual, and spiritual healing, which are essentially vibrational and higher energy medicines; and thus, too, will religion and spirituality re-acquire their basic therapeutic nature and role. This new conception also assumes that health involves growth and evolution—dynamism—rather than homeostasis and equilibrium, that is, maintaining the status quo. Any threat or block to the growth and evolution of the person, as well as any major frustration of the will and loss of meaning can, in itself, be considered pathogenic.

Hence the most essential problem is to find the means to preserve or restore health, so let us begin by asking, first of all, what is "health"? Health is simply the proper alignment, or connection between all of the seven bodies of a person. (They are also called the "seven vehicles of life and consciousness".) Health is the ability to know, to be, to feel, and to express in action and deeds one's full Self on all planes of being—and this implies the right functioning of each body and the right connection between all bodies. In functional terms, it is what the Greeks called "*Harmonia*," and the early Christians, "Peace." Moreover, this condition is not static but dynamic, involving growth, evolution, and self-actualization.

On the physical level, health involves physical strength, coordination, and the ability of our biological organism to do what we ask of it without pain or strain. On the emotional level, it involves courage, looking forward to the day ahead and all of its challenges, being eager to live, to face challenges and adventures, to express oneself, discovering and realizing one's true nature. On the mental level, it involves a clear perception and understanding of what is in the world and in oneself: making sense of one's daily experience. It means having a clear, perceptive, and effective mind, which is the opposite of confusion. On the spiritual level, it involves the proper functioning of intuition, inspiration, and discernment. It means knowing and wanting to do God's Will in concert with, rather than exclusively out of, our ego or our human self. It also means faith, in the sense of:

a. Realizing that everything has meaning, purpose, and order, and that these are, ultimately, good and working for our own growth and self-actualization and that God is working through the universe and ourselves.

b. Being able to focus and express our will (through concentration), our thinking (through meditation) and our feelings (through devotion). This means being able to direct to a specific point (in ourselves or in the world) all of our attention and creative energies, all of our love and emotions, and all of our knowledge and ideas.

When we take all of these dimensions together, on all planes, "health" then means "*la joie de vivre*," the joy of being alive, the ability to be and express oneself fully and consciously, and to consciously complete our evolution and destiny. It means being what we are meant to be, which can only be fully realized when we have achieved union with God, or the proper alignment and integration of the human with the spiritual Self.

I will never forget the trip that I took from Florence to San Giovanni Rotondo, in Southern Italy, for my first meeting with

Padre Pio. On that memorable trip I learned many things and had experiences I still remember even though it was more than thirty years ago. To visit and spend some time with a saint, or a spiritually awakened person, is always a little pilgrimage, a microcosm of life itself, with all of its adventures, misadventure, and surprises. To begin with, just to be in the presence of such a person is an "experience" in itself. It has a deep and subtle impact upon one's whole being and consciousness. Thus, it is a way of "self-discovery," as well as discovery of the world. Moreover, most "happenings" and experiences—the things one lives and learns—seem to have a definite purpose and to be part of a larger plan, which may truly unfold and unveil itself only later in life.

My first "lesson" occurred even before I arrived in San Giovanni. As I was driving to San Giovanni Rotondo, I noticed something interesting that had happened countless times before, but which I had never noticed in the way I did then. It was simply that as I increased the speed of my car the air resistance also increased. This made me think and became the symbol for something much more important. There is a great paradox and a seeming injustice in life. Many people who appear to be innocent go through a great deal of sufferings and tribulations that would seem totally undeserved and unjust. Not only that, but many people who are spiritually awakened or who have greatly contributed to human welfare, in one fashion or another, seem to be carrying a much heavier load of sufferings, injustices, and tribulations than most people. I could not help thinking about Jesus, all He did for the world and how the world treated Him. I also remembered the saying: "Before you get a 'crown of glory,' you will get a 'crown of thorns.' " What does this have to do with the fact that as one increases one's speed on a highway, the air resistance also increases? It is an analogy, I believe, on the physical plane of what also happens on the human plane, namely, in increasing the process of one's evolution, one faces a condensation of experiences over a short period of time, and therefore, one faces more "pressure," "tests," and suffering. This principle, as well as the fact that nothing ever happens by chance or in vain and that all human experiences have a cause and a purpose when seen from the spiritual standpoint, has made it much easier for me to accept my own trials, tribulations, and sufferings without immediately being able to grasp and comprehend their purpose and function.

An important lesson I learned, while I was with Padre Pio in San Giovanni Rotondo, is that not all illnesses can or are meant to be healed; and that it is not the healing in itself that is the most important thing, but rather understanding God's Will, the lessons one has come in this world to learn, and what one has come to do in this world. There are times when one must learn to live and accept a certain illness or handicap as well as times when one must do everything in one's power to overcome it and heal it. This principle is connected with one of the Ten Commandments, "Thou shalt honor thy father and thy mother," that is, one must enter into a right relationship with the "male" and "female" principles of one's being. It was indelibly impressed upon my consciousness through the following strange case history.

A man who suffered from terrible insomnia had come to see Padre Pio; he also had an undefined sense of guilt about being a "failure in life"—of having "thrown his life away." He had also had a very bad and painful skin disease and had gone to many dermatologists and experts, but to no avail. Finally, he resorted to a "healer" who told him that he could be cured in about ten sessions of "therapeutic touch." The man accepted, went to the "healer," and was healed in less than two weeks. However, within a period of three weeks, he began to develop strange, new symptoms—insomnia, a sense of failure or guilt, of having missed the purpose of his life. As time went by, the symptoms became more intense and he began again to look for a medical solution. As he could not find one, either with traditional medicine and psychotherapy, or with alternative methods, he decided to come and see Padre Pio.

Clearly Padre Pio felt that I had something to learn, as he allowed me to be present at their meeting. Padre Pio told the man that he could do nothing for him—or for anyone, for that matter—except to pray for him that God's Will be done. He asked him whether he was ready to accept God's Will. The man said yes, but Padre Pio, looking at him with piercing eyes, told him "No, you are not!" and sent him away. I was truly shocked. How could a "saint" refuse something to someone, especially to pray to God for him? But the man came back the next day, told Padre Pio he was ready to accept

God's Will and to please pray for him. Once again, Padre Pio told him he was not ready and sent him away. I could not believe what my eyes saw and what my ears heard! Finally, the man came a third time, still begging Padre Pio to pray for him; and this time he did! The man returned and went down on his knees to thank Padre Pio for his prayers that had, apparently been heard and answered as his symptoms began to disappear. Then, the man left and I never saw him again. Padre Pio told me, however, that the old skin disease would soon reappear and that the man would have to live with it. Apparently his soul had chosen this type of experience for certain lessons the man had to learn and that we could not understand.

When the man had gone to the "healer," who used his own will and energies to remove the skin disease, to remove this test and lesson chosen by his soul, the higher consciousness of the man let him know in its own language—insomnia, the sense of guilt and "failure," that he *was* missing what he had come in this world to do. This is how I learned concretely and practically that not all diseases are meant to be removed and that the most important thing is not healing per se, but to know and be able to carry out God's Will (and that a saint can behave in a seemingly strange and incomprehensible way!).

What is disease or pathology? It is simply the opposite or the lack of health. It is first and foremost being a stranger to one's self, being cut off from the spiritual Self—being an alien to one's self (which, interestingly enough, is the true etymological meaning of "disaster"). It is not knowing who we are, where we come from, where we are going, or why we are here, why certain things happen to us, what we should do, or what God and life expect from us. It is to have lost our "peace," our "harmony," our very self, and thus grace, or Divine Light and Life. It is being separated from God and from our divine Spark.

On the physical level, disease involves an energy deficit, a dysfunction, tension, or breakdown of one or more organs or organ systems, which may or may not involve pain. On the emotional level, it involves fear, anxiety, tension, suffering, and an emotional roller coaster that has gotten out of control, adversely conditioning our consciousness and behavior. It also implies ceasing to love ourselves, and ceasing to love life with its challenges and adventures—the desire to run away, fall asleep, and avoid daily experience. It may imply becoming ruled by or addicted to compulsive self-destructive relationships. Behind all of these symptoms, it may also involve a "short-circuit" within our Heart Center, our astral body, and the inner flow of the life forces.

On the mental level, it involves confusion, a blurred perception of reality and of our experiences in the world and within ourselves, and a lack of understanding what is happening, why and what we should do about it. This cognitive darkness and confusion can lead us to make costly mistakes, perpetuate dysfunctional patterns, and become passive and demoralized, lost or cut adrift on the sea of life.

On the spiritual level, disease means being cut off from our higher Self, from our inner source of intuition and inspiration, from the very inner spring of life, love, and knowledge. It is truly being *disgraziato,* as the Italians say, "cut off from grace." It manifests as lack of faith, despair, imbalance, and separation.

Moreover, while the spiritual Self and the spiritual bodies cannot be sick in themselves, they can be short-circuited, separated from, or misaligned, with the other vehicles or bodies. It is this separation or short circuit that constitutes the essence of disease or pathology. So long as grace, light, or spiritual energies can flow through our vehicles and reach the human self or ego, we may, indeed, be limited, restricted, deprived of something important, or experience pain, but we will never fall into the emotional, mental, and spiritual darkness of not knowing what is happening and what we should do and into the agony of despair and utter confusion.

Thus healing, true, holistic, and complete healing always involves working down the planes from the spiritual to the physical level. It involves re-establishing the link and proper alignment between the spiritual and the human self and between the soul and the personality, enabling the Light and the spiritual Energies to flow freely between them in an open circuit, recreating and harmonizing each body on its own level and through its laws. Hence, it does use conventional medicine (allopathy) as well as alternative therapies (naturopathy, homeopathy, acupuncture, etc.) and psychic and spiritual healing (laying-on-of-hands, praying, and visiting sanctuaries).

It is interesting to note that the great work, as also true religion, has two essential aims: to heal the sick and to enlighten those who are in darkness. By degrees, human consciousness may be changed and exalted, and through this expansion of consciousness, a person may first become aware of and then unite with the Spirit within. The most complete and effective series of spiritual exercises put together for that purpose is, in my experience, the divine Liturgy, or Mass, and the older Healing Service in the Catholic traditions.

Both the Mass and the Healing Service operate as integrated series of psychospiritual exercises and operations to heal the sick, to enlighten the ignorant, and to bring more Light to us so as to cause a change and an expansion in our consciousness. But they do it in different manners and with different emphases. The Mass focuses primarily on spiritual enlightenment, by communing with Christ, and secondarily on healing our various sicknesses, while the Healing Service focuses primarily on healing, through the operation of the spiritual light, and secondarily on enlightenment. The first is a preliminary step for the second, and the second is the true culmination of the first.

In terms of sequence, we could say that the Healing Service precedes and is a preparatory step for the Mass, which is why the former is celebrated on Saturdays and the latter on Sundays. These two major rituals, however, should be seen as being inwardly related and complementary to each other. The first aims at bringing the sick to the level where true spiritual enlightenment and growth can begin, while the second aims to help those who are well and normal to evolve and grow to a higher spiritual level.

Briefly put, the Healing Service aims at healing all of our diseases and deficiencies, and at making us whole. This involves psychospiritual operations, using our human efforts, the theurgic work of the officiant, and the Light, Consciousness, and Energy transformations of the Healing Angels that are present, the cosmo-telluric energies of the sanctuary, and the free outpouring of Divine Light, which is the curative agent in this process. The work of the angels, of the officiant, and of the individual, together with the energies of the sanctuary, all assist in opening channels for and amplifying our sensitivity to the Divine Light that is invoked and that flows from the altar and from our inner Tree of Life.

The operations of the Healing Service are neither a purely

material nor a purely spiritual process but a psychospiritual one; they do not involve physiological exercises or transformations as much as a transformation of human consciousness. For it is through such an alternation and expansion of human consciousness that these psychospiritual operations affect both the physical and the psychospiritual processes of our being, and that they are projected into the psychic atmosphere of the place where we are.

The Healing services of the Catholic Traditions do contain in their operations and make available to the individual the famed Panacea, the universal medicine capable of healing, by degrees and in time, all human diseases. Let us now continue our esoteric analysis and explanation by asking the following questions: What kinds of diseases can the human being fall prey to? What is the panacea and how does it operate? And who and in what manner can the Healing Service heal?

What kind of disease can human beings fall prey to?

Human diseases are as many and as varied as are human beings themselves, yet they do fall into certain broad categories:

1. Physical diseases;
2. Emotional diseases;
3. Mental diseases;
4. Spiritual diseases;
5. Diseases that prevent us from coping with our normal tasks in life and with coping with reality as it is socially defined;
6. Malfunctioning, stresses, and tendencies that will eventually result in disease that will make us unable to cope with our normal tasks in life;
7. Immaturity, incompleteness, and blindness that prevent our spiritual Self from manifesting itself and our whole nature from being on the material plane what it is on the spiritual planes.

At the core of all diseases, we find precisely what the etymology of the word signifies: a "*dis-ease*," a "lack of harmony," a break and disruption in the alignment of our various vehicles and their faculties, especially with respect to the divine Spark. To heal on all levels, therefore, implies restoring that harmony, that proper alignment between the divine Spark and Its vehicles, which is what spiritual harmony, or the "peace that passeth human understanding," truly is.

Let us take an obvious example from the physical plane. Should a block, stress, or injury prevent the circulation of blood, lymph, or nervous energy, the affected organs and cells that are cut off would begin to fall sick, that is, to cease their proper operations and, eventually, decay. In order to function, to remain vital and alive, they must remain properly aligned with the rest of the organism, or in harmony with the whole.

We find the same principle at work at the level of the emotions and of the mind. Psychopathology is essentially **dissociation**, the dissociation of cognition and affect, of affect and conation (meaning volition or voluntary action), and of cognition and conation; or it is the dissociation of the subjective and the objective levels of reality—between what one is and what one claims to be, between what one says and what one does—so that the lower elements end up by ruling the higher, thus breaking up the proper alignment.

Finally, on the spiritual level, we do not have diseases proper but rather blindness, or the inability for the Spirit to express itself, to manifest its attributes and its life-giving force. And this, once again, can be seen as a lack of proper integration between man's various vehicles, between his various human faculties and his spiritual Self.

If disease is a disharmony, a break in the proper alignment of man's vehicles and of their systems, then healing is, essentially, the restoration of that harmony, the achievement of peace, or the realignment and proper coordination of the human bodies, their faculties, and the divine Spark. In that manner, and in that manner alone, can spiritual, mental, emotional, and physical diseases be truly healed; any malfunctioning, stresses, and tendencies that would result in disease are corrected in time, and immaturity, incompleteness, and blindness made whole.

What is the Panacea and how does it operate?

The panacea, or universal medicine, is the *Divine White Light of the Spirit.* Its basic modalities and expressions are the following:

1. It operates by flowing down the planes, from the spiritual to the physical, and by restoring harmony, proper alignment, true peace, and real psychosynthesis between the human bodies or vehicles, their faculties, and the divine Spark.
2. In order for Divine Light to flow through a person's being, there must be an outpouring of energy from above answering the call and longing of human effort from below. There must be, in other words, an opening at the spiritual level, an opening at the physical level, and a proper set of channels at the psychic levels.
3. The path that the Divine Light follows in its outpouring from the spiritual to the physical level corresponds with that of the Tree of Life where its various "receptors" are the psychic and spiritual centers or *Sephiroth.*
4. It is the Tree of Life in each of us (and its various centers) that is to be activated, unclogged, balanced, and lit up in order for the Light and Life of the Spirit to truly flow through us and heal us at all levels.
5. In these terms, this is the central purpose of the Healing Service: to light up, activate, and coordinate the various centers on the Tree of Life so that true and lasting healing may take place on the different planes.
6. Furthermore, this is what each of the prayers, petitions, and formulae of the Healing Service can help to accomplish—most of the time without even the candidate being aware of what is transpiring on the inner and higher planes.
7. This is why the Head Center (Kether, the point of spiritual contact), the Heart Center (Tipphereth, the central prism or distributor of Light), and the Feet Center (Malkuth, the point of physical contact) are so important and why so many prayers and formulae of the Healing Service stimulate them into activity.
8. The importance of participating actively in a Healing Service

and reproducing the service of the temple in our own consciousness and aura is so that the Light first flows within, from one's Divine Spark, before we can then be receptive and open to the Light and healing that come from without. Should this not happen, the Light projected from the altar and by the officiant and the healing angels would simply flow around us without penetrating inside of us, where the alchemical transmutation and expansion of consciousness takes place.

9. Finally, this is also why relaxation, whether physical (neuromuscular) or psychological (the release of worries, stress, and anxiety), is so important for truly effective spiritual work. Relaxation induces a partial expression of true harmony, peace, and of the correct alignment of the vehicles, their faculties, and the divine Spark.

Who and in what manner can the Healing Service heal?

In the macrocosm, following the line of the Greater Mysteries, the Divine White Light originates in the Holy Trinity (the infinite ocean of Life and Light). Then it flows through the Celestial Hierarchies all the way down to the two healing angels that always minister at all duly consecrated altars. Thus, through the healing angels and the officiant, the Light is projected through the temple and the Tree of Life of all those who are present and participating in the service. This takes place on the visible and on the invisible planes, and is extended to the city, to nature, and to the whole world as a stream of purifying, healing, and elevating energy that is grounded by the cosmo-telluric forces of the earth and of the place where the temple or church happens to be.

Within human consciousness, in the microcosm of our aura, following the line of the lesser mysteries, the Divine Light begins in the Head Center (Kether), then it flows to the Heart Center (Tipphereth) via its transformation in the Cheek and Shoulder Centers (Chockmah and Binah, Chesed and Geburah). From there it flows to the Sexual Center (Yesod) via the Hip Centers (Netzach and Hod), and is "grounded" in the Feet Center (Malkuth). On its downward and outward path, the Light heals, vivifies, and reintegrates all that which it comes in contact with—to the extent that receptivity and openness to it exists.

In the macrocosm, the Divine Light re-establishes the Great Chain of Being—harmony with the celestial and terrestrial hierarchies. In the microcosm, it re-establishes true psychosynthesis, or the proper alignment of the human bodies or vehicles, with their faculties, and the Divine Spark. It also blazes open, both in the macrocosm and in the microcosm, a path, a Ladder of Jacob, through which man and God, the conscious and the superconscious can be reconnected and fused into one.

Each who is present and participating in the Healing Service, or whose name is mentioned at the Altar, receives just as much Light, therefore just as much healing, as he or she is asking for, is ready to receive, and is able to use properly. Healing can then take place at the spiritual, mental, emotional, and even the physical level—at the level of prophylactic intervention or even at the level of enhancing our wellness and the growth and actualization of our being. It is not only we who are healed but also the world in which we live and all those with whom we come into contact as our aura has been filled with Light which is now radiating in its turn.

Sometimes, however, we may not get the specific healing we ask for when we ask for it. Whether we do depends on Divine Purpose, our faith, and our destiny. Yet if we pray and participate with all the faith we can muster, some healing and help will always come—be it no more than understanding and having the strength to accept our present illness and to see Divine Purpose and valuable lesson to learn in it.

In summary, the Healing Service of the Catholic traditions can be described as:

1. One of the two most complete, practical, and effective rituals of the Christian Church, the central aim of which is healing on all planes leading to spiritual enlightenment.

2. A down-pouring of Divine Light answering a call and effort from below, which produces a progressive transformation and expansion of human consciousness.

3. A complete and well-integrated series of formulae to practice

and develop concentration, meditation, and contemplation, as well as a complete series of spiritual exercises.

4. A practical, safe, and effective method of activating, cleansing, equilibrating, and lighting up the whole Tree of Life.

5. A practical, safe, and effective way of altering and expanding human consciousness.

6. A practical and effective way of communing with the spiritual Self, the Christ within.

7. A practical and effective way of obtaining balanced, safe, and integrated healing for oneself, for others, and for the world.

8. A practical, safe, and constructive way of coming in contact with the inner worlds, the Celestial Hierarchies, and the Communion of Saints.

9. A simple, effective, and safe way of consciously assisting one's spiritual evolution and of actualizing, in an integrated fashion, our most important human and spiritual faculties.

10. A simple, effective, and safe way of applying the teachings of the spiritual traditions in one's daily life.

The invoked Light comes down through the Planes, via the Celestial Hierarchies and the Officiant, in the macrocosm, and through the Tree of Life in the Microcosm, being then, in both cases, "grounded" by the cosmo-telluric energies of the earth and of the Sanctuary. Then, it blends into the collective atmosphere of the Temple and our aura (or "Sphere of Sensation"). From there, it is projected unto those whose names are invoked and into the atmosphere of the surrounding area, bringing healing and enlightenment to those who "seek it" and who are "on the same wavelength." Therefore, it requires our total participation, which will lead each one of us to make our unique contributions by adding to the healing "stream" by the refraction of the Light in one's Tree of Life and by playing his own unique instrument, his distinctive Soul-note and frequency.

One should not forget that light and energy also flow "up" from the earth, through the subtle network of cosmo-telluric currents that are channeled by rock and water. This can explain why there are special places where sanctuaries are built (e.g. Chartres, Lourdes, St. Anne de Beaupres) sometimes on the every spot where earlier religions also built or had a special sanctuary or Holy Place.

It is when we have the threefold juncture of strong and alive cosmo-telluric Energies, Angelic Presences and Energies, and the right inner preparation and devotion of the candidate, that the Tree of Life becomes an incandescent *filament* and that the aura is filled with Light and Energies. It is then that true healing take place—in the most natural way.

Having analyzed health and disease from a spiritual and esoteric viewpoint, it should be clear that there is as deep and intimate a connection between sin and disease as there is between healing and salvation. For it is sin or transgression both individual and collective, that brings about disease and sickness, just as it is salvation that brings about holistic health.

Exoterically, sin is, generally, connected with morality as it implies the transgression of a divine commandment. From an esoteric viewpoint, when we transgress basic universal and spiritual laws and principles (going "across" rather than "with" evolution) we cut ourselves off from our source and our self, and thus lose Light, Energy, Life, and Health. This means that we lose the ability to do what we want until we change our ways, enter again the flow of evolution, and pick up where we left off—or "die" to start anew. Hence, there is a limit to both sin and evil, as their ultimate consequence is death. But from every mistake a lesson can be learned and from every failure a success can be born, as God can and does redeem all human mistakes and errors—in due time.

Salvation, therefore, means something very different esoterically than exoterically. In the latter, it can mean belonging to a certain religion or church, living by their moral code and precepts, accepting Jesus as our personal Savior, etc. This should lead us when we die to enter heaven and eternal happiness and to be reunited with God and with our true Self. From an esoteric perspective, however, it can mean to be in a state of grace, filled with Light and properly connected and aligned with all of our bodies, their faculties, and the spiritual Self, so that we can consciously direct our attention, vital energies, and resources, our thoughts, feelings, and faculties, to further our growth and evolution. Simply put, it means to cooperate consciously and direct our efforts, energies, and resources to further accelerate our growth and becoming. It means to be and do what God wants us to be and do, period! Within this state, which can be achieved at one point and time of our earthly lives, we shall know intuitively what to do and what not to do, how to be patient, and how to rejoice in the ineffable gift of Life, and in the unspeakable marvels that await us along the way and at the end of our journey.

CHAPTER SEVEN

The Priest and the Initiate in the New Era

In the Piscean Age, wherein evolution occurred through the clash and conflict of opposites, the Priest and the Initiate stood in sharp contrast to each other. The Priest represented tradition, the preservation of the past and of its revelation and Mysteries, and acted as the "agent for maintaining the status quo," as Max Weber pointed out. The Initiate (the spiritually awakened person who can as well be a Prophet, Saint, Seer, or Sage), on the other hand, represented the life force and visions in his own experience the new revelation, and acted as the agent for social change. In the Piscean Age such forces for change were often persecuted or even killed, being perceived as great threats to the established order. In the coming Aquarian Age, these two former opposites, Priest and Initiate, will be reconciled, working out a greater and a larger synthesis than either could have done separately.

Today there is a great deal of discussion and debate about the "New Era" or the "New Age," an idea that has almost become an "ideological trademark," with very positive connotations for some and very negative for others (with the term "Aquarian Age" giving something of an "astrological floor" to it). What do these terms really mean? What are the implications of living at the onset of a new Age? One of my Italian publishers is actually called *Eta dell'Acquario* (the Age of Aquarius) and its logo depicts a young man pouring water over the earth, which, to me, embodies the core feature of this New Era. This figure is really the opening of the Heart Center, the awakening and pouring of Love unto one's spiritual Self, others, and the world. It represents coming out of the desert of separatism, egoism, the idolatry of the mind and the senses. It also represents the passage from analysis to synthesis, the moving to a global village with a planetary consciousness, and to the awakening of spiritual consciousness.

It means that tribal religion is passing away, together with materialism, reductionism, and rationalism, to lead the way to a truly universal religion with an emphasis on intuition and wholism. This New Era has both a subjective and an objective aspect: It must begin in the consciousness, the awakened consciousness, of every individual, to then be lived and objectified in one's words, deeds, relationships, and our entire environment. Thus we can say that for some it already exists, for others it is now being born, while for still others, it has not come yet. Most important, in order for it to come much depends on us, on each and every one of us, on what we love, what we do, and how we treat each other. For it is *we*, both individually and collectively, who must give birth to the Aquarian Age, first in our consciousness, then in our words and actions, and finally, in the world. What it involves, basically, is a transformation of our consciousness and a paradigm shift in our knowledge. But its true flowering will come only when we recognize experientially that we are all the offspring of the same God, that we are all "brothers and sisters," and that what we do unto others we do unto ourselves.

The New Age will involve the primacy of love over knowledge and power, of spiritual consciousness over technical knowledge, and of good relationships over career and possessions. It represents the "graduation" of humanity from "adolescence" into "adulthood," wherein we will know who we are, where we come from, where we are going, and what we come to accomplish on earth. Thus, we will become responsible for what we are, where we are going, and how we will get there. In my opinion it will involve a transformation as great and radical as when human beings left nature to enter society and emancipated themselves from the bondage to their instincts and biopsychic drives; except that this time it will be from ignorance, fear, confusion, and illness that we will emancipate ourselves, to become aware of God's plan for us, individually and collectively, and thus to be able *consciously* to cooperate with it. Above all, it will be the era in which Love will be reborn and will regain its primacy in our lives.

Indeed, today we need both the Priest and the Initiate, for the Priest is the guardian and the carrier of the "letter" of the sacred traditions while the Initiate is the vehicle and channel for the spirit that vivifies the letter of the sacred traditions. The letter needs to be vivified and reinterpreted with different meanings, implications and applications, at different times for different people who stand on different levels of consciousness, lest it be "cut off from the spirit" and misleading to those who take it literally. In other words, in the coming age, it will be realized that both the letter and its carrier (the Priest), and its soul (the meanings, implications and applications given in that letter) with its carrier (the Initiate) are necessary to reach and reactivate the spirit of the sacred traditions—Spiritual Initiation with its personal experiences and inner realizations.

No church or spiritual organization could exist in the physical world if it had to depend on Initiates alone to make it function, for the simple reason that there are not enough of them in the world. And human beings need people who are on their own levels of consciousness and being to present and interpret the visions and revelations that constitute the essence of the sacred traditions and of religion. They also need people who are further ahead and who can act as models or revealers of what they, too, shall one day be.

I remember the time I went to San Giovanni Rotondo in Southern Italy, to meet Padre Pio. Besides Padre Pio, I also met scientists, medical doctors, priests, monks, and "ordinary people." I discussed many subjects and issues with them, including the work, powers, and special "knowledge" of Padre Pio. I was struck by the large variety of viewpoints and answers I got. I encountered nearly the whole vertical axis of the levels of consciousness. I also noticed that it was not the most advanced, sophisticated, or comprehensive answers people sought and found most meaningful, but rather, those that truly corresponded to their own level of consciousness and personal experience. The implication of this is simple and clear: we need people on different levels of consciousness and being to present and interpret the core symbols, images, archetypes, myths, and rituals of the sacred traditions.

Most people, including the various ranks of the clergy, lack the personal experience and have little idea of the "inner side" of church services. To get a glimpse, we may be able to observe Initiates as they participate in the rituals (communion in particular) or discuss with them their own visions, experiences, and interpretations on higher levels of consciousness. It is in this fashion that Initiates constitute a prototype and a model, a "point of reference," as it were, for our own future achievements. Yet what is crucial is not so much to have ecstasies, visions, or peak experiences—beautiful and enlivening as these may be—as to be motivated to do the work, to pour one's whole being—one's attention and vital energies, one's mind and thoughts, and one's love and feelings—into the rituals and what we are doing. This is the inner secret of the essential mechanism for making the elevator of our vertical axis of consciousness move up or down, altering our level of consciousness and making the work and prayers truly come alive. It is here that the presence and experiences of initiates, acting as genuine spiritual mothers and fathers, can be of invaluable assistance: first, by the very energies and vibrations they radiate; second, by their living witness of what happens on higher levels of consciousness; and finally, by what they can tell us of their own experiences and interpretations of the body of the sacred traditions and of their particular religion.

From the standpoint of the sociology of religion, religion as a whole is seen as resting upon five basic structural parts:

1. A belief system, the intellectual-cognitive component—its essential beliefs, conception of reality, and philosophy of life;
2. A system of practices, the will-action component—what they do, the rituals, prayers, spiritual exercises, and various practices;
3. An ethical system—the fundamental moral principles upheld and taught;
4. A social organization—how people relate to the clergy and to each other, in a structured hierarchical fashion or in an unstructured, egalitarian fashion;
5. A system of personal experiences—the visions, ecstasies, and

inner experiences that are the fruit of living this religion and of practicing certain spiritual exercises or rituals.

In the Western religions, Judaism and Christianity in particular, the weak pillar of the above series is, unquestionably, the last one, the system of personal experiences. As Dion Fortune tells us:

> In our materialistic age we deny and ignore many things that were known to the companions of our Lord and the prophets before Him, who knew and relied upon the ministry of angels. What are these angelic beings who relieved the necessities of our Lord after His temptation in the wilderness, who warned God's servants of impending danger, and released the apostles from prison?
>
> May it not be that there are states of existence about which our five physical senses tell us nothing, and that, as the Bible implies, there are indeed organized and intelligent forces, of both good and evil, which we cannot perceive, yet which nevertheless influence us profoundly?
>
> We shall never understand the mystery of the world unless we recognize this underside of existence. It is the clue to a very great deal that baffles us. The angels of His presence dwell there, also the devils of the evil imaginings of men's hearts. It is upon this, the mind side of things, that we must seek for the realities and potencies that underlie our world of appearances.[1]

This situation, in my opinion, is deeply related to the absence of spiritual mothers and fathers, elders, or Initiates who can provide discipline and exercises and can supervise the unfolding of the consciousness and the growth of the candidate . . . leading to "personal experiences." This may also be one of the reasons why so many bright, motivated, and spiritually hungry people have gone over to the Eastern religions, yogas, or esoteric approaches (mysticism, occultism, magic, the hermetic, Qabalistic and Rosicrucian traditions). This is because they provide the discipline, training, and personal experiences their souls crave. This is the fundamental function and void that the Initiate will fulfill in the future—and is already fulfilling for a small number of people.

This system of personal experiences and realizations, based on the transformation of consciousness, the raising of vibrations, and the activation of the psychospiritual Centers, is rooted in and emerges from the Western Initiation system. All genuine Initiates pass through this system, or a similar one, either directly and consciously or indirectly and unconsciously, to achieve its distinctive characteristics. This system is composed of the four "Elemental Initiations" and of the three "Spiritual Initiations" that are linked to the seven ranks of Holy Orders (described in the chapter on the Sacraments in *Divine Light and Fire*). The genuine Holy Orders in the Catholic Christian traditions are based upon the ageless Initiation system and provide the essential insights and exercises necessary to achieve consciously the seven fundamental Initiations. This does not imply that a Priest is an Initiate, or even that he knows what the Initiation system is all about, or even that it exists. Yet all the essential symbols, images, archetypes, and exercises to achieve each one of the Initiations is provided in the sevenfold hierarchy of Holy Orders. Hence, the Priest can either prepare himself to achieve any initiation grade or guide others to achieve these without himself achieving the same grade.

In essence, the Western Initiation system approaches human nature in a holistic fashion and aims at giving those who undergo it and live it comprehensive self-knowledge, self-mastery, and self-integration, both at the personality and at the Soul level. Thus, the whole person, with all of her or his powers, levels, and faculties, is progressively unveiled and revealed so that, by degrees, the person may know, be, and express herself or himself consciously and fully, and fulfill his or her destiny on earth.

Life itself, with all its joys and sorrows, trials and vicissitudes, is actually a great and comprehensive path of initiation. It is a long and winding road, often steep or narrow, but nevertheless leading those who tread to the same great end. The initiation system is a much more direct path on which, once a person achieves a minimum of personal awareness, motivation, and ability to work on himself or herself, one can consciously move to affect one's evolution. Its fundamental requirement is a full and conscious participation in its process, involving one's whole being and life. To gain everything (i.e. one's true Self and its full expression in creation) one must risk everything, and become completely involved.

The Western Initiation system is grounded in the Tree of Life and its Centers, Energies, and levels of consciousness. Hence, it does involve an understanding of and working ability with the universal Qabalah. It begins with the knowledge, mastery, and proper care of the physical body and its vitality. Then it moves on to the knowledge and control of the will, the imagination (with which the will is closely connected), and the ability to make decisions and act—to choose between good and evil. The next step is to gain knowledge of and mastery over one's emotions and to learn how to express them and integrate them with the rest of the psyche. Finally, at the level of the personality and of the elemental initiations, we gain knowledge and mastery over the mind and learn how to use it properly. At this point, the personality, the temple and vehicle of the soul and of the self—of life, love, and creativity—has been prepared and is ready for its greater and more conscious "ensoulment" by the soul and the Divine Spark. Thus we come to the three spiritual and final initiations, the purpose of which is to enable the self-actualized person to act in the world and to fulfill its purpose and destiny—God's Will and Plan for that person in this life.

The first spiritual Initiation deals with activating and using the *intuition,* and the inspirational flow coming from above. It deals with the illumination of the mind and the connection and then union between the lower and concrete mind and the higher and abstract mind. This process finally reveals to the initiate who he is, where he come from, where he is going, and what is his purpose in this world. It unveils God's Will and plan so that one can act consciously to accomplish one's mission in the world. It deals with what the French aptly call "*L'Intelligence du Coeur,*" which has "reasons" that reason does not understand.

The second spiritual initiation deals with activating and illuminating the *heart* and the higher emotions—with the expression of spiritual, higher, or altruistic love. As such, it requires the proper integration of mercy and severity, of expansion and contraction, and of the male and female polarities within oneself and then in the world. It also involves being able to do and act for the true and higher good and welfare of others and not simply to gratify their ego or live up to their expectations. Finally, it enables a person to become a real and living light for others and for the world—to channel the Divine Light or "Grace" in this world and to be able to transmute evil into good, which is a genuine alchemical operation.

The third and final spiritual Initiation deals with activating and illuminating the *will* of the candidate to consciously and completely align it and harmonize it with the Will of the Divine Spark and, through the Divine Spark, with the Will of God. Thus, when the Adept has successfully passed the third spiritual Initiation, he become a clear and undistorted channel for the Will of God on earth and acts as His instrument in the physical world. At this point, which is the highest spiritual achievement one can aspire to while incarnate in a human body, it is no longer *my* will but the Will of the Father that is accomplished. This truly sums up the greatest and highest spiritual attainment of a human being who can then truly know God and do His Will, which is also the Will of his own true Spiritual Self. To move beyond this point would imply dying and ascending to a higher level of being and vibration which is yet invisible and which is represented, in the Catholic traditions, by the mystery of the Ascension.

In the new era, and already today for those who are ready and who have achieved this stage, religion will be represented and carried out on earth through three major ministers or carriers: The priest for its body, the spiritually awakened philosopher for its soul, and the initiate for its soul and Spirit. Each will act on a different level to complement and complete the others. Religion moreover will also become fully universal, linked with the new planetary consciousness and teaching that we are all sons and daughters of one God and thus brothers and sisters in the highest, spiritual, and ontological sense. It will also be grounded upon a sound, practical, and experimental metaphysics wherein direct vision and personal experience will play a most important part—a part that is the distinctive feature of the "religion of the Holy Spirit," the new phase or level of religion. Thus will a new consciousness and a new behavior lead to a new society and a new world, with possibilities and realizations we can now but wish for, to be born in us and in our midst.

In this new "heaven" (state of consciousness, attitudes, and knowledge) and new "earth" (world and society), human beings will be guided (by their own conscience, teachers, friends and families, and by Priests and Initiates) to unfold a personal philosophy and art of living that correspond to their own level of consciousness and being, character, and aspirations. Through this philosophy and art of living they will be able consciously to cooperate with the creation of their own being and the fulfillment of their destiny. Some will be chosen to evolve faster and to take more pressure and make greater efforts and sacrifices while other will evolve in a slower fashion, making fewer efforts and sacrifices. But all will be led, by various teachings, different approaches, and personal examples to answer the fundamental questions of life: Who am I, where do I come from, where am I going, what have I come in this world to accomplish, and what is the meaning of my daily experiences? What value system and ethical system should I live by? Should I marry and, if so, how can I find and choose the right mate? What kind of work (vocation) and hobby (avocation) should I do and how can I find out what work I should do? And what is the right kind of spiritual discipline for me to live by, to best accomplish my purpose on earth, to develop and unfold the best and highest in myself, that I may make my greatest contribution to others and, thereby, live the most creative, constructive, and happy life?

Religion will again become the sacred science of reconnecting and binding together all the various parts of one's own consciousness and being, and then oneself with God, with nature, and finally with other human beings. This will reconstitute the Great Chain of Being, linking Heaven and Earth, Spirit and Matter, and God with His Creation, bringing about that Peace, Justice, and Harmony that have always been the secret longing of conscious and mature human beings.

Then the greatest enemy of human kind, the internal and external "Devil," will finally be unmasked and conquered. That is, we will assume a full control over the core functions of our psyche—thinking, feeling, willing, and imagination in particular. This will enable us to "exorcise" or transmute negative thoughts, feelings, words, and deeds into positive and constructive ones. Neurotic fears, anxieties, desires, cravings, passions, frustrations, anger, jealousy, impatience, worry, and hurry will finally be conquered as one conquers a wild horse or animal. Diseases and illnesses, accidents, successes and failures, life and death, good and evil, male and female, joy and sorrow—the whole spectrum of human states, emotions, and experiences will be transfigured. Every person will be shown the future that awaits them, where all are the children of God with the same potentialities. The Communion of Saints will become a reality, accessible to those who climb the various rungs of initiation and who expand their consciousness and raise their vibrations. Life on earth will be perceived as a gigantic school with extraordinary possibilities for growth, self-actualization, Self-realization, and personal expression. And then the "lamb" will walk with the "lion."

Exactly when this will come about and how many people will realize this and live it as a reality I do not know. But I do know that this is coming about—and coming about fast—because, as has been said by many people, "the twenty-first century will be spiritual or it will not be at all!" With the power, knowledge, and sensibility that we now have at our disposal we can create or destroy with much more power and at a more rapid rate than at any time before (which, paradoxically, greatly limits our essential options). We can either move onto a higher and qualitatively different level of consciousness wherein we will witness and live the Birth of Spiritual Consciousness within our own hearts and souls and experience the coming of the Messiah, the Savior . . . or destroy ourselves.

My vision of our future is very close to that of the Gospel of Thomas. The hidden will become revealed (the esoteric become exoteric), the male will be reconciled with the female, heaven will be linked with earth (thus spirit reconnected with matter and God with Man), and the inner will be manifesting in the outer (namely, the higher states of consciousness will be expressed in full, waking consciousness). It is in this situation that the poor will be reconciled with the rich, the sick with the healthy, the beautiful with the ugly, the strong with the weak, and the priest with the initiate, for all will be enveloped and propelled by the irresistible force of human and divine *love.* For it is love alone that, when consciously realized and manifested, can reconcile opposites and bind the entire creation with its Creator. Love is the beginning, the middle, and the end—the fundamental power and the ultimate realization—of Initiation, of *genuine, living,* and *authentic* initiation. Today, initiation is becoming more and more the highest aspiration and the most lofty goal of life on earth for a growing number of human beings. This is the call of direct and personal spiritual experience that can only be understood if it is *lived* as opposed to intellectually described; and so this might be a good place to conclude my attempt at the latter and give time and room for the former . . . in the silence of the reader's own consciousness.

Conclusion

With this volume, I feel as if I have given birth to a spiritual child, a child representing the very best and highest in myself. I believe I have achieved what I came into this world to do; and therefore, I feel that "peace profound that passeth human understanding," that inner and indescribable feeling of personal fulfillment and joy that comes from accomplishing one's duty to the best of one's ability.

The end of this book marks the end of a very long and important cycle in my life. But it also marks the beginning of a new cycle, one filled with more wonders and surprises, more adventures and challenges—the challenge to climb higher, to love more passionately, to achieve greater things I can't even perceive yet but can vaguely intuit in my moments of greatest relaxation and inspiration.

I hope this book also marks a beginning for you, the reader—the beginning of new possibilities for experimentation by approaching your life from a different angle. With genuine interest and commitment, some creative insight and imagination, and a lot of hard work, you can reap the benefits of this approach, benefits that are enormous at all levels but most particularly at the cognitive, emotional, and vital levels.

Viewed together with *Divine Light and Fire*, this work presents an organic whole that draws from the spiritual traditions of the past (Catholic Christianity in particular) as well as from the latest advances of modern science and from the most creative breakthroughs of our time. It offers both a cognitive framework and a practical discipline and set of psychospiritual exercises to lead us to live fuller, more constructive, more creative lives—to make sense of life, to answer the fundamental questions of life, to grow consciously and responsibly, and to find both Self and God, the Living Source and Essence of Life, Love, and Wisdom. It does this by taking us right back to the living core and essence of our Western spiritual tradition and to the religion of our birth, whatever that tradition and religion may be. The same esoteric spiritual perspective, however, can also be applied to other churches and religions and their living essences.

This work integrates graphically and symbolically the exoteric and esoteric aspects of the Christian Catholic tradition. It gives the majestic bird of psyche (human consciousness) its two necessary and complementary wings: the wing of tradition and the wing of direct personal vision and experience. Human consciousness can only soar to its highest levels of potential and possibility with both wings, for in these wings together dwell the answers to the riddle of being, to the riddle of the universe, to the riddle of life, to the riddle of all reality.

The actual work, the realization of the Great Work, the birth of genuine spiritual consciousness or the coming of the Savior, depends upon your own readiness, training, aspirations, and personal experiences; for the ultimate Reality and Self we call God is, in the last analysis, always a personal lived experience, a passionate love. It is never an intellectual discussion, never reading or writing a book. This is the true meaning and implication of the authentic esoteric perspective. It can only be a personally realized and lived experience.

The rest is up to you. Now you have a roadmap. Use it and share it with others so that more Light, more Love, more Joy, will flow into your consciousness and into your being and thus into the world. I suspect this is what Christianity was and is all about.

APPENDIX A

The Tree of Life and the Psychospiritual Centers

In several chapters of this book, I have mentioned the psychospiritual Centers of man's energy and consciousness fields. These Centers, their nomenclature, nature, implications, and correspondences, constitute a very important and fascinating, albeit complex and controversial, subject matter that cannot adequately be covered in this work. To do justice to this subject, another book is the minimum that can be expected and which I already have in the planning stage for a later time. In the Western Spiritual Tradition, this subject is related mainly to the Qabalah and the Ten Sephiroth of the Tree of Life. In the East, on the other hand, it is related to the Chakras. Excellent works have been published on this topic and can be consulted by the interested reader. The ones that I am acquainted with and consider most reliable, both in theoretical and in practical terms are:

Dion Fortune, *The Mystical Qabalah,* London: Ernest Benn, 1963.

Gareth Knight, *A Practical Guide to Qabalistic Symbolism,* London: Helios Book, 1965.

Z'ev ben Shimon Halevi, *Tree of Life,* New York: Samuel Weiser, 1973.

Z'ev ben Shimon Halevi, *Adam and the Kabbalistic Tree,* New York: Samuel Weiser, 1974.

Israel Regardie, *The Tree of Life,* New York: Samuel Weiser, 1973.

William Gray, *The Ladder of Lights,* London: Helios Book, 1968.

R.G. Torrens, *The Golden Dawn,* New York: Samuel Weiser, 1973.

C.W. Leadbeater, *The Chakras,* London: Theosophical Press, 1938.

For the practical purposes of this work, I will include a basic diagram of the Tree of Life and list the Hebrew and English names of the Centers together with their most important meanings and correspondences.

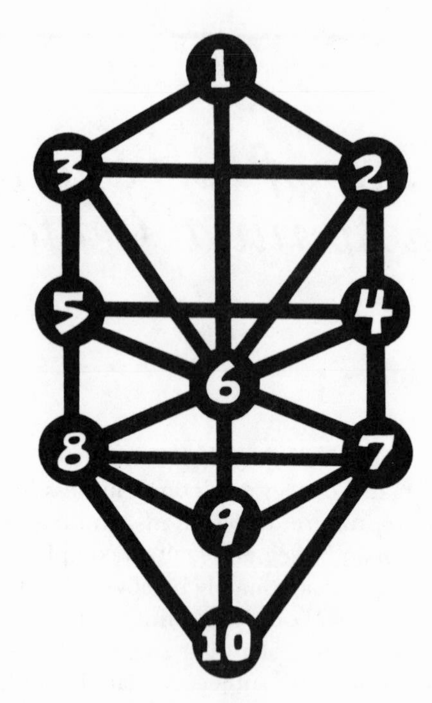

Figure A: The Tree of Life

Name of the Centers	Location on Human Body	Astrological Signs
1. Kether, The Crown	Head	Primum Mobile
2. Chockmah, Wisdom	Left Cheek	Zodiac
3. Binah, Understanding	Right Cheek	Saturn
4. Chesed, mercy	Left Shoulder	Jupiter
5. Geburah, Severity or Strength	Right Shoulder	Mars
6. Tipphereth, Beauty or Equilibrium	Heart	Sun
7. Netzach, Victory	Left Hip	Venus
8. Hod, Splendor	Right Hip	Mercury
9. Yesod, Foundation	Genitals	Moon
10. Malkuth, Kingdom	Feet	Earth

Key Correspondences

1. **Kether:** Point of contact with the Divine Spark, Unity.
2. **Chokmah:** Eternal Masculine Principle, Expansion.
3. **Binah:** Eternal Feminine Principle, Contraction.
4. **Chesed:** Principle of expanding life, Energy, Enthusiasm.
5. **Geburah:** Principle of contracting life, Order, Discipline.

6. **Tipphereth:** Intuition, Equilibrium.
7. **Netzach:** Emotion, Combination.
8. **Hod:** Thought, Separation.
9. **Yesod:** Vitality, Creativity, Conception.
10. **Malkuth:** Behavior, Resolution.

Spiritual Experience, Virtue and Vice linked with given Center

1. **Kether:** Union with God; Completion of the Great Work; none.
2. **Chokmah:** Vision of God; Devotion, none.
3. **Binah:** Vision of Sorrow; Silence; Avarice.
4. **Chesed:** Vision of Love; Obedience; Tyranny, Hypocrisy.
5. **Geburah:** Vision of Power; Courage; Cruelty.
6. **Tipphereth:** Vision of Harmony; Devotion to Great Work; Pride.
7. **Netzach:** Vision of Beauty; Unselfishness; Lust.
8. **Hod:** Vision of Splendor, Illuminations; Truthfulness; Falsehood, Dishonesty.
9. **Yesod:** Vision of the Machinery of the Universe; Independence; Idleness.
10. **Malkuth:** Vision of Holy Guardian Angel; Discrimination; Inertia.

The Tree of Life with its Ten Sephiroth has its roots and being in the Four Worlds of the Qabalists. These are:
Aziluth: Divine World; Divine Consciousness.
Briah: Mental World: Superconscious.
Yetzirah: Astral World; Conscious.
Assiah: Physical World; Unconscious.

The basic task of the student of the Mysteries is to become acquainted with the Tree of Life and each of its psychospiritual Centers; to cleanse, activate, and coordinate their energies so that these can be consciously used by the Self in man's consciousness and actions.

APPENDIX B

The Muscles of Human Consciousness

It has now been over 30 years that I have been active in the Human Potential Movement, the "Consciousness circuit", and various Esoteric Groups, both as a leader and as a participant. I have attended and been a lecturer at a great number of symposia and lectures, and have joined many psychological and spiritual groups dedicated to human growth and spiritual development, as the *Leitmotiv* of my personal and professional life has always been "the study of human nature for its conscious development" or "the expansion of human consciousness and the achievement of spiritual consciousness." I used to have a great deal of enthusiasm and very high hopes and expectations for this kind of endeavor and for the people I would meet at these gatherings and who joined these groups. While my enthusiasm for and dedication to human development and spiritual awakening have remained and, in fact, grown and intensified over the years, my hopes and expectations for what people could actually achieve by attending these groups, symposia, and lectures have considerably diminished. For, I noticed that, just as in the world where most people seek financial wealth and social status but few actually achieve it (about 5% according to the latest statistics), so in the consciousness circuit, great are the hopes and promises but few are the results. Most people attend symposia after symposia, lecture after lecture, taking various courses and applying different techniques, or they join one or more esoteric or spiritual organization or they find and follow one more guru but soon settle down in a new routine with very little changes in their lives and beings. Many lectures and several years later, they are still basically where they were before in terms of their everyday lives, state of consciousness, and level of being. The only thing that really happened is that they found and accepted a few new ideas and beliefs to meditate upon and to discuss with their friends; ideas and beliefs such as reincarnation, the subtle bodies, the psychospiritual centers, the various auras, more evolved human beings, meditation, prayer, and ritual. As these have remained in their head and have not descended into their hearts or been "enfleshed" in their lives—in other words, as they have basically heard, read, or discussed these ideas and beliefs but not *felt them* or *incarnated them,* little has actually happened in their lives and beings and not much basic change really occurred. Many of these people will later either fall into a given routine of mechanically reaffirming certain ideas and principles, with no actual connection with their real lives or they will become disenchanted and drop out altogether from the consciousness circuit and become disillusioned and disappointed in the spiritual quest as many other people have become disillusioned or burned out in the quest for money and status. A most interesting book to read along these lines is Robert de Ropp's *Warrior's Way,* which is his own personal "spiritual biography" and odyssey through many New Age groups and spiritual organizations. The basic question one can ask at this point is, What has gone wrong? Why have so many high ideals and lofty objectives failed to deliver what they promised?

The answer to this fundamental question came to me, by analogy, when one day I was reflecting upon my diary and meditating on what happened to a dear friend of mine and myself in the Summer of 1958, and it came in a genuine flash of intuition that illuminated a most important principle for me and provided the foundation for this essay. At that time, my friend and I were students at the University of Denver, and we had been invited by my parents to spend the summer in Europe. During that academic year, we had worked very hard on our course work and, being quite ambitious, in our quest to make the Dean's List and to achieve academic distinction, we had completely neglected our physical bodies, doing no exercise or sport, eating and drinking too much, and leading a very sedentary and intellectual life—a very unbalanced life. My parents, who knew what was going on, at least in my case, were very eager that we use the summer to get back in good physical shape and get involved with different sports to achieve this. To this end, they provided us with the best available instructors for snow-skiing in Switzerland, water-skiing on the Italian Riviera, and for playing tennis. Our instructors were, indeed, excellent and very dedicated persons, but all their efforts availed naught! We could see what they were doing; we understood what they were telling us; and we could have written superb papers on the principles and techniques involved in all three sports. But *our bodies were absolutely not capable of following through and of doing what our minds and wills were telling them to do.* It was at this point that the Swiss ski instructor told us, in a flash of intuition and recognition, "Boys, you are in bad physical shape! Before you do anything else and waste your time and mine, go and build and coordinate your physical muscles."

This, of course, was the answer. For over a month we did just that. We went to a gymnasium and learned and practiced all kinds of physical exercises designed to build and coordinate our physical muscles until they got back in good shape. Then, we went back to our old instructors and were able to carry out their instructions and to have our bodies do what they were told to do, and thus we learned a much better technical snow-skiing, water-skiing, and tennis. A breakthrough had occurred, which broke the deadlock into which we had fallen and which opened the door we wanted to get into. The same breakthrough happened to me later as I was considering the psychological and spiritual blocks or dead-ends into which so many people have fallen, and provided me with the answer to the basic question I raised before; "What went wrong with all these spiritual idealists and enthusiasts?"

The answer is, of course, Do we not also have consciousness or psychospiritual muscles? and, Should not these muscles also be trained and coordinated before we can expect any kind of genuine change and growth to occur in our consciousness and being? Naturally, we do have such muscles, so that the basic question becomes, "What are these muscles and how can they be properly developed and coordinated so that they can be applied in human growth and spiritual awakening?" To answer these questions, in a disciplined and systematic way, we must first ask ourselves, "What is *human* consciousness and what are its structure and functions?" Just as if we wanted to develop and coordinate physical muscles we should first ask ourselves the question, "What is our *physical* body and its anatomy and physiology?" The latest model of the human psyche is, as far as I am concerned, that proposed by Psychosynthesis developed by Roberto Assagioli. In formulating and then articulating the now famous "Egg of Psychosynthesis," describing the structure of the psyche, and the "Star or Flower of Psychosynthesis," describing the functions of the psyche, Assagioli has put together the most comprehensive, up-to-date, and sophisticated model of the human psyche. In a nutshell, the structure of the psyche is composed of 7 basic elements which are The Human Self, the Spiritual Self, the Field of Consciousness, the Preconscious, the Subconscious, the Unconscious, and the Superconscious—while the functions of the psyche are also seven; namely, Willing, Thinking, Feeling, Intuition, Imagination, Biopsychic Drives or Impulses, and Sensations.

The central thesis and basic postulate of this lecture is that the most important muscles of our consciousness are those associated with willing, thinking, feeling, imagination, and intuition. And that these muscles are just as important for mundane or physical endeavors as they are for psychological or cultural endeavors and for spiritual endeavors. These, in other words, are the core psychospiritual tools for successful living and for the expansion of human consciousness and spiritual awakening. Without a minimum amount of training and coordination of these muscles no exercise, technique, or consciousness raising and spiritual development program can truly get underway, let alone succeed! For as the Spiritual Tradition has rightly put it in a nutshell, "First, we must know something, then we must feel it, and only at that point can we live it in order to become it." These muscles of our consciousness or, as I have called them, "the core psychospiritual tools for successful living" are truly the ABC, the foundation for all conscious change and personal growth on any level. These are:

1. Concentration associated with willing or the "focused energies of the self," the "ability to say 'yes' and to say 'no' to ourselves and to others" or, in other words, to know what we want and to know what we don't want. The Will can be compared to a battery that can be charged as well as discharged and Concentration is, in itself, a science and an art.
2. Meditation associated with thinking or "thinking in a focused and disciplined way about any subject, mundane, human, or spiritual." And Meditation can also be considered a science and an art that has to be properly understood and mastered.
3. Devotion associated with feeling or "directing one's emotions and opening one's heart and energizing whatever subject one is concerned with." The ability to express devotion or to put one's heart into a subject of one's choice is science and an art that has to be cultivated and developed.
4. Visualization associated with imagination or "the ability to create images or symbols to represent what one is concerned with" and allow these images and symbols to "come alive" and to unfold in one's consciousness. To visualize properly is, likewise, a science and an art which are now being rediscovered with the study and application of "mental imagery."
5. Invocation-Evocation associated with intuition or "the ability to focus all of one's attention or concentration, one's thinking or meditation, one's feeling or devotion, and one's imagination or

visualization upon a given topic or subject and then empty one's consciousness to receive the energies and impressions that might then flow into it at that point." The proper training of the intuition and the mastery of invocation-evocation is not only a science and an art but, perhaps, the most important psychospiritual work one can do to contact one's Higher Self and obtain guidance and conscience from within in these turbulent times when all external authorities and experts are slowly crumbling!

Concentration, Meditation, Devotion, Visualization, and Invocation-Evocation must be cultivated and developed first individually and then concomitantly when one reaches the stage of training of the Intuition which requires the previous mastery and coordination of the first four to enable one to work with Invocation-Evocation. What Religion and the Spiritual Traditions call faith and to which they give so much importance is really a Triangle of the focused and coordinated use of Concentration-Will, Meditation-thinking, and Devotion-feeling ("Thou shalt love the Lord Thy God with all thy heart, all thy mind, and all thy soul") with the visualization of the proper images and symbols at its base. The image of the Pyramid can also be used wherein the four corners and angles of the Pyramid represent, respectively, Concentration-Willing, Meditation-Thinking, Devotion-Feeling, and Visualization-Imagination, which thrust upward toward the top and point of the Pyramid, forming a grand Invocation, to be answered by Evocation—then descend in the center of the Pyramid as true Inspiration or Intuitive Insight and Energy.

The final question I will address myself to in this lecture is how can we concretely and practically develop and train in ourselves and apply in our daily lives these "muscles of our consciousness" or "core psychospiritual tools," first individually and then collectively and simultaneously in the opening of the Intuition? Obviously, each one could be the object of an entire lecture and even a book, so I shall try to be brief and focus upon only a few of the most important guidelines and exercises that will enable each of you to use your own personal experience of the reality and development of each of these "muscles" and "tools."

1. Training of the Will and Concentration: The Will is the key function of the psyche as it relates the energies of the self to all the other functions. It is neither a great deal of raw energy nor a blind determination to do what one wants to do at any cost. Rather, like the director of a play, the Will focuses, directs, and utilizes all the energies and resources of one's consciousness and of one's human environment to achieve the goals and objectives that are wanted

and focused upon. More than a physical or biopsychic energy, the Will is a psychospiritual energy, the energy of life of the self, working through the psyche and the biological organism to accomplish and realize one's objectives. As such, it is the key to one's freedom and integrity as a human being.

a. Learn to focus upon, or concentrate upon, a physical object, then a feeling, a thought, an image, and finally a symbol or a basic theme.
b. Learn how to say "no" to others, to desires and longings in yourself, and to various inducements of circumstances, no matter what the attraction or the temptations offered—for, whenever we resist ourselves or others, or deny ourselves, we charge our will and, conversely, whenever we "give in" to temptations and desires, and seek "instant gratification," we weaken our will.
c. Learn to reflect upon and determine what you really want and don't want and then make sure that you pursue what you want and avoid what you don't want. Never abandon a plan, project, or undertaking you have carefully selected and in which you believe because of the difficulties or the time involved. If something is worth starting, it is worth completing.

2. Training of Thinking and Meditation: Thinking is getting a cognitive grasp of the outer and inner universe. It implies developing thoughts and ideas about what exists and what is happening both outside and inside of our being so that we can become more conscious of outer and inner reality and make sense out of them. Here, it is vital to remember a most important psychological law: the psychospiritual energies of the psyche will follow and energize whatever we are thinking about or directing our thoughts toward. Indeed, we become what we think or contemplate! Meditation is the process by which we think in a systematic and disciplined way and it involves 3 basic inner aspects: reflective, receptive, and contemplative meditation.

   Reflective meditation involves organizing all our thoughts, ideas, and experiences—all that we know, have learned and experienced—about a given subject in a clear, coherent, and integrated way. It means bringing all the materials that pertain to our chosen subject from the subconscious and the preconscious into the field of consciousness so that we can "behold them" and become aware of them.

   Receptive meditation involves clearing and emptying our minds of all our acquired knowledge and experience about our chosen subject so that new insights, associations, and information may be received. Here, the main process is to "let go," to relax and become fully receptive, once our attention has been fixed upon a given subject.

Contemplative meditation is the spiritual dimension of meditation. It follows the first two steps and involves expanding our state of consciousness, through a chosen spiritual exercise, so that we can now "behold" our chosen subject in an altered state of consciousness, "become at-one with it," and let the materials pertaining to it now flow from the superconscious into the field of consciousness. It is "inspired and intuitive thinking" about our given subject so that new aspects and insights may be gathered from the superconscious and the Divine Spark.

The topics one can choose for meditation are as many and as wide as life itself; they can be qualities such as joy, courage, peace, love, wisdom; the symbols of basic prayers such as Heaven, Father, Kingdom, or a whole prayer; life goals and plans or the ideal model of a personality one would like to develop.

3. Training of Feeling and Devotion: While willing produces energy and life, thinking yields knowledge and understanding, feeling awakens love and the ability to have and to express deep emotions, or to "feel deeply" about whatever we focus our attention upon. Life, knowledge and love are truly the "food of our inner being" and indispensable components for any person to be properly equilibrated, psychologically integrated and humanly fulfilled—to be able to live as a full human being.

Feeling is the ability to evoke emotions, to feel deeply and passionately about something, to be truly moved from the heart by whatever we focus our attention upon.

Devotion is the process of expressing and focusing emotions and feelings about a given subject of our choice. To feel deeply and passionately about something we must involve our will, images, thoughts, and symbols that stir up something in our make-up and that will open the doors of the Deep Mind.

What we need is a good meditation on our own emotions; what does and does not "move us." Then, we must discover and utilize the images, thoughts, symbols, and the particular situations and relationships that evoke profound and genuine feelings from us. Through prayer and beauty we can also energize and amplify the quality and intensity of our emotional responses. The name of a person, the image of someone we love or really admire, the recall of a particularly emotionally charged event—all of these can be powerful helps to cultivate devotion.

4. Training of Imagination and Visualization: Just as the power of observation is crucial to gather knowledge about the physical world and to orient ourselves in that world, so the power of inner observation, or visualization is crucial to gather knowledge of the inner worlds.

   The imagination is the image-making faculty and visualization is the power to see things with the "eye of the mind." Imagination has both a "female," or reproductive nature, and a "male," or creative nature (the ability to reproduce on the "screen of the mind" anything one has seen or experienced and the ability to create new things, events, or stories). The imagination and the power of visualization have an immense evocative and awakening power for our emotions, thoughts, and even our intuition, by resonating with and opening up the various regions of the psyche (the subconscious, unconscious, and superconscious) with their related energies, vibrations, and states of consciousness. The essence of visualization is full concentration and absorption in the fantasy one is living which acts as the key to unlock the doors of the unconscious and of the superconscious.

   The basic exercise to develop the imagination and the power of visualization is "guided imagery" or the "inward journey," for, just as we can take journeys in the outer, physical world, so we can also take inward journeys in the psychological and spiritual worlds of the psyche. The most important "inward journeys" involve:

   a. Taking a trip to the sea and exploring its depths; taking a trip to a mountain to find the Temple of Silence or the Temple of the Sun, or a Guardian of the Mysteries; and taking a trip under the earth to explore its caverns and depths.
   b. Encounters with other beings during the trip—human, animal, or angelic, and dialoguing with them, giving them something and receiving a present from them.
   c. One can take these beings with oneself in moving through the psychological space going up or down, and watching for transformations that are likely to occur in them or in oneself.

   While one is taking an "inward journey," it is very important to study oneself and to observe any changes that may occur in one's state of consciousness, and to be able to describe them. One should also bear in mind that every being and event encountered represents, analogically, a part of one's being and life.

5. Training of Intuition and Invocation-Evocation: Concentration, Meditation, Devotion, and Visualization are the central psychological "muscles" or "tools" which form the base from which the 5th,

Intuition, with its twin processes or Invocation-Evocation, is to emerge to crown the whole edifice.

Intuition means "seeing from within" of the "teachings from within." It is the bridge or channel that links up the field of consciousness with the superconscious, and the human self with the spiritual Self. This is why it is the only faculty that is half psychological and half spiritual in nature and that links up the psychological with the spiritual dimension of our being like a true "ladder of Jacob." Genuine spiritual Illumination, true spiritual Initiation, or Divine Revelation, must all come through the channel of the intuition which must be open for such purpose. For once the channel of the intuition is open and the spiritual Energies (the Light, Fire, and Life of the spiritual Self) can flow through it, they will enliven, quicken, and bring to life all the other functions and literally transform man's consciousness, translating him from the realm of nature to the Kingdom of God. Then, and only then, will a person be guided from within and receive all the answers to the most basic questions and problems of life from his own Higher Self rather than from various external experts and authorities!

To activate and open up the Intuition a sequential process known and Invocation-Evocation is used. In Invocation, the first 4 functions of the psyche—willing, thinking, feeling, and imagination—are used in a synchronous fashion so as to concentrate all our attention upon the Spiritual Self residing in our "Head-Center," direct all our thoughts and meditations to Him, send Him all our love and feelings, and visualize Him in our favorite image or symbol. This creates an upward-thrusting triangle with Concentration and Meditation at the outer two triangles, Devotion at the center, and Visualization at the base. Another basic image or model that can be used is that of the Pyramid where Concentration, Meditation, Devotion, and Visualization form the 4 angles meeting at the top from which Evocation or the Intuitive Energies flow down the center of the Pyramid. When this is done to the best of our present abilities, Invocation will be answered by Evocation which is the down-pouring of spiritual Energies into our field of consciousness wherein spiritual Life energizes our human will and concentration, spiritual Light illuminates our meditation and thinking, spiritual Fire warms and expands our feelings and devotion, and spiritual Vision opens up and crowns our visualization. Ultimately, however, it is important to remember that Intuition with its accompanying Inspiration and Revelation are spiritual gifts and not human or psychological achievements. As such, a life of devoted prayer, selfless service to others, and proper perspective and balance in all the things one does, is, perhaps, the best way to obtain the gift of true Intuition which only the spiritual Self can bestow.

The core exercises to develop and train the Intuition are:

1. Guided Imagery, the Inward Journey: ascent in psychological space and meeting/dialogue with a Sage, an Angel, the Light, or the Sun.
2. Inner Dialogue: conversation with a symbol of the Superconscious and/or the spiritual Self.
3. Letter to the Higher Self: expressing aspirations, fears, and needs.
4. Prayer: practice of Silence and Ritual to maximize sensitivity and receptivity and the down-pouring of Light and the spiritual Energies.

Crucial here is also to learn how to listen to and recognize the "voice of Intuition" when it does manifest itself and to cultivate Peace, or systematic relaxation, and Life, or systematic stimulation, in our whole personality.

APPENDIX C

The Art of Living at the End of the 20th Century

Of all the arts, and there are many, the art of living is certainly the most important, the least known and practiced, and today the most needed, as it corresponds to and answers emergent and vital and imperative needs and aspirations of our times. It is clear to most people that our life and problems are becoming ever more complex; that our consciousness is expanding towards both the depths and the heights; that we are experiencing, in an alternating and exacerbating cycle, devitalization and a chronic fatigue as well as an "implosion" of psychospiritual energies and a great intensification of our sensitivity. At the same time, we are witnessing the greatest breakthroughs in modern Western medicine and the appearance of entirely new and baffling diseases, of which AIDS is but the best known and most tragic case. Economically, we are experiencing the fifth generation of computers and the first generation of robotics while, at the same time, we are on the brink of one of the major economic crises of this century which could greatly reduce our standards of living. In this situation, it is becoming increasingly clear that a conscious art of living suited to our nature and emergent needs and aspirations, is becoming a vital necessity. With the demographic explosion and the appearance of "overchoice" together with the distinguishing features and tendencies of our age (see my *Apocalypse Now,* Llewellyn Publications, 1988), the only way that we will be able, not only to actualize our potential and faculties, but to literally survive at the *human* level, is to develop and implement a comprehensive philosophy and an art of living.

Today, you and I are standing in the very midst of the Great Passage of the transition between our adolescence and our adulthood, between the Piscean and the Aquarian Age, in which humanity will become more and more conscious, alive, and powerful—for good as well as for evil. Thus a multidimensional, interdisciplinary, and conscious philosophy and art of living are, indeed, the Great Challenge of our times. In my trips to and work in many countries (the USA, Canada, France, Italy, Switzerland, and Spain in particular), in reading and meditating upon the literature of many disciplines (sociology, psychology, anthropology, psychotherapy, medicine, as well as the emergent parapsychology, esoterism, and spirituality), I have found some essential ideas, fragments, and germs leading towards the systematic unfolding of such a philosophy and art of living—but not yet its final structure which in any case must be a personal realization.

In the last five thousand years, and especially since the Renaissance in the West, human evolution has gone through an enormous transformation, a qualitative metamorphosis. In leaving nature to enter society, human beings have transformed their consciousness and their becoming—beginning with a slow and external unconscious evolution to now arrive at an internal and ever-accelerating conscious evolution. In simple words, this means that, today, if we want to acquire certain things or, especially, become something, realize certain objectives, we must involve our *whole selves* to realize and incarnate our dreams and visions. It is no longer God or nature, or even society and its institutions, that will assume and insure our being and our becoming—it is *ourselves* who must do it, as frightful and painful as this may seem to many. This must start with the inside of our being and consciousness and arrive at an external materialization and objectification. This, perhaps, is the esoteric reason why all great social and cultural institutions and traditions, all traditional values, and all external reference points are beginning to dissolve and disappear—why the great beings, saints, sages, and masters are hiding, slipping into the background, and leaving public life. To enable us to change our basic attitude towards life and ourselves—to change the focus of our attention and of our efforts from extraversion to introversion and from infraversion to supraversion. And that the words "liberty", "responsibility", and "integrity", as well as "assume control over your being and your life," are becoming the key terms of humanistic psychology and of the Human Potential movement with the New Age consciousness. It is in the framework of our present conditions and expansion of human consciousness that this philosophy and art of living, with its integration of new perceptions, intuitions, and realizations, becomes necessity—necessity that will become all the more imperative as we pass from the empire of the head to that of the heart, from analysis to synthesis, and from a reductionistic and alienating materialism to an integrating and vivifying spirituality. St. Augustine had this experience. His visions of Christ disappeared and out of the darkness he heard Christ say to him, "I have disappeared right before your eyes in order for you to return into your heart to find me."

It is clear that an art of living is not a science and must thus be adapted, refined, and personalized by each person, taking into account his or her level of consciousness, values, and personal experiences. And yet there are basic laws, principles, and core intuitions that could form the skeleton or substance of this philosophy and art of living—reference points and points of departure that must then be adapted and personalized for each person at his or her particular situation and moment of life and development. It is these laws, principles, and central intuitions that I would now like to discuss with you and that constitute the heart of this reflection. It is also these essential insights that will constitute the foundation of the integral or holistic education of the future, the seeds of which have already been planted with some burgeons beginning to appear, here and there, in different disciplines and in various countries. In its essential structure, this philosophy and art of living rest upon the following points:

1. A general theory of human nature: What is a "human being"?
2. A specific model of the psyche: What is "human consciousness"?
3. The vital principles of holistic and preventive medicine, which are now emerging.
4. A personal autobiography with its continuation in a journal of our personal life, work, and growth.
5. A theory and personal application of the love of God, worship, or prayer.
6. A theory and personal application of the love of our fellow humans, of "good will in action", or of service.
7. A psychospiritual discipline to be followed, alone and in a group—the formation of a "love vitamin generator", of a "circle of light", of a "living church for the New Age" which I have called "the Noah's Ark of our Age" or the "Spiritual Family."

The development and articulation of each of the "seven dimensions," or "core aspects" of this philosophy and art of living can be found in my many books, articles, and lectures. In summary they seek

1. To get to the very heart or quintessence of the reality of things.
2. To connect and integrate these things into a larger framework, which I call a "comprehensive philosophy of life" and a "holistic art of living" for our age. Please bear in mind that this philosophy and this art, in each of its seven vital dimensions, must go through the five stages of incarnated wisdom, that is:
   a. To be properly intellectually understood and synthesized

b. To descend from the Head into the Heart, thus, to be not only intellectually grasped and understood, but also emotionally felt.
c. To be wanted by the will.
d. To be lived in our consciousness, our being, and our daily life.
e. To live this reality by becoming one with it.

A. A general theory of human nature

1. That a human being is a true microcosm of the microcosm—a synthesis of all of reality, a Child of God
2. That a human being is not yet a completed being, but a being-in-becoming, who must now know himself, master himself, and integrate himself so as to consciously complete himself
3. That a human being is not yet a "unified and integrated being," that he remains a multidimensional being on his way to completion. As such, human beings have
   a. A biopsychic nature, the physical body
   b. A human nature, his Psyche or Soul, composed of several subtle energy bodies which are still unfolding (the etheric, astral, mental, and spiritual bodies)
   c. A spiritual nature, the Divine Spark, the as yet unknown Self
4. The Great Work and challenge of our Age, and of all times, has always been that of actualizing and realizing our psychosocial nature, our human consciousness, to harmonize it with our physical bodies and with the Divine Spark, to become, in this way, a Temple of the Living God, which involves the Second Coming of Christ in our Heart, Soul, and Being

B. A specific Model of the Psyche, the old Hindu science of the Antahkarana, the specific structure and functions of human consciousness

a. The structure of the Psyche, the "Egg of Psychosynthesis" with its seven structural component parts: the human self, the spiritual Self, the field of consciousness, the preconscious, the subconscious, the unconscious, and the superconscious
b. The functions of the Psyche, the "Star of Psychosynthesis": willing, thinking, feeling, intuition, imagination, biopsychic drives, and sensations
c. The essential work of the individual consists in knowing, exploring, and mastering the seven functions of the Psyche with the energies as well as in making the whole "Egg" or Unconscious, Conscious.

C. To know and to be able to live by the seven basic Principles of holistic and preventive medicine, that is

1. Nutrition—knowing how to feed oneself
2. Sleep—getting good quality and the right quantity of sleep
3. Physical exercise—getting the right kind and enough of it
4. Sexual and love life—to know and be able to direct one's sexual and emotional life
5. Emotional and intellectual life—to know, feed, and manage them properly
6. Social life—understand it and be able to organize it properly (Love Vitamin Generator, Circle of Light, Spiritual Family)
7. Spiritual life—to know and be able to feed one's Soul: worship and prayer

D. Write an autobiography and then continue it with a journal. Include

1. What has happened to us (female polarity)
2. What have we caused to happen by our own acts and words (male polarity)
3. The events that we have lived (external, objective polarity)
4. Our way of perceiving, defining, and reacting to the events we have lived (internal, subjective polarity, the true axis of human and spiritual growth)
5. Our human relationships with the persons who are most important to us (psychosocial network)
6. The events we consider crucial for us in their psychological order
7. What we have learned, understood, felt, loved, wanted, and created

Then, continue this autobiography by keeping a journal organized in the same fashion, along with a workbook describing the work or exercises done, when, and with what results.
E. A theory and personal application of the Love of God, in worship, and prayer

1. Choice of the appropriate techniques: Using Images, Symbols, and Rituals as consciousness and energy transformers. The nature and the use of the Divine Names, of the Sign of the Cross, the Our Father, the Hail Mary, or the recitation of the Ten Commandments.
2. Knowing and having developed the "Muscles of Human Consciousness" and the techniques necessary to make prayer "hot" and "alive," an agent for psychospiritual transformation: Concentration, Meditation, Devotion, Visualization, Invocation-Evocation;

developing Faith and activating the psychospiritual Centers

3. Integrating the timing and sequence of prayer with other activities

F. A theory and personal application of the love of our fellow humans, of "good will in action," or of service

1. Choice of a vocation and avocation to utilize one's energies, train one's faculties, and express one's self in work that is useful to others: studies, profession, contributions
2. Expression of good will, hobbies and volunteer work to enrich others and oneself. To feel and live the fact that to "serve others is to serve God and one's Self—to express love"
3. Integrating and timing and sequence of service with other activities (work, prayer, and relaxation)

G. A psychospiritual discipline to be followed alone and in a group

1. To make the right kind of choice of a discipline or "path" to be followed daily. To create one's "growth and life project" that corresponds to one's nature and to the present period of one's life
2. To alternate, in a harmonious fashion, between the polarities of personal work and group work, spiritual and physical, emotional and mental, work and play, desire and duty
3. To create or join a "work group" or a "Spiritual Family"

The very heart and essence of a philosophy and an art of living consist in

1. Knowing oneself, accepting oneself, integrating oneself, and perfecting oneself *in all the parts and aspects of one's being and consciousness* in the heights as well as the depths, in the Light as well as in the Shadow, *without exceptions*
2. Hence, to be able to know, accept, integrate, and perfect *all the parts and aspects* of the Universe and of Life, both high and low, *without exceptions*
3. This will enable the true "philosopher" and "artist of the art of living" to live without fears, worries, anxieties, remorse, guilt, or cravings, in full appreciation of oneself, of life and its trials, with gratitude towards God for the gift of life and the *Joie de Vivre* (which, for me, is the true meaning of a full, conscious, and adult life!)

Developing a comprehensive philosophy of life and art of living is one way of consciously finding peace, harmony, and the right relation between all the parts of one's being and all the parts of creation. One must also be able to discern properly the right measure, the right proportion, the right distance, and the right timing. This is not easy to achieve and can probably not be realized in just one life on earth. Yet this is our final destiny, such as I see it at this point. It is the goal towards which all my efforts and aspirations are directed; for it is, in this art of living that one can find the Philosopher's Stone (the key to true knowledge), the *Elixir Vitae* (the key to conscious immortality), and the *Panacea* (the universal medicine) that is authentic Holiness manifesting itself by an explosion of new and vivifying energies culminating in the *Joie de Vivre*! The philosophy and art of living is the "perennial philosophy" seeking the wisdom of God. The art of living is to live in God's presence—in the presence of love, consciously manifest in our lives.

Notes

CHAPTER 1: THE ROMAN CATHOLIC MASS

1. Underhill, Evelyn. *Worship*, p. 22.
2. Roche de Cappens, *The Nature and Use of Ritual.*
3. Ibid.
4. For more details, see the chapter on the Creed in *The Nature and use of Ritual for Spiritual Attainment.*
5. Underhill, Evelyn. *Worship*, p. 138.
6. Rahner, Karl. *Theological Investigations*, Vol. 4., p. 331.
7. For greater details, see the chapters on the Lord's Prayer in *The Nature and Use of Ritual for Spiritual Attainment* and *The Invisible Temple.*

CHAPTER 2: LEVELS ON THE VERTICAL AXIS ON CONSCIOUSNESS

1. Underhill, Evelyn. *Practical Mysticism*, p. 154.

CHAPTER 3: A JOURNEY INTO THE INNER CHURCH

1. Underhill, Evelyn. *Worship*, p. ix–xi.
2. Fortune, Dion. *Mystical Meditations on the Collects*, p. 119.
3. Underhill, Evelyn. *Practical Mysticism*, p. 36.
4. Ibid., p. 83.
5. Ibid. pp. 143–44.

CHAPTER 4: THE ROLE OF PRAYER IN ESOTERIC CHRISTIANITY

1. Underhill, Evelyn. *Practical Mysticism*, pp. 30–31.
2. Carrell, Alexis. *L'Homme c'est Inconnu.* Paris: Plan, 1946, pp. 138–139.
3. Keating, Thomas. *Open Heart, Open Mind*, pp. 19–20.
4. Roche de Coppens, Peter. *The Nature and Use of Ritual for Spiritual Attainment, The Invisible Temple,* and *Apocalypse Now.*
5. Underhill, Evelyn. *Practical Mysticism*, p. 159.
6. Ibid., p. 96.

CHAPTER 5: PILGRIMAGE: THE INNER AND OUTER JOURNEY TO THE HOLY PLACE

1. Charpentier, Louis, *Les Mysteres de la Cathedrale de Chartres.* Paris: Robert Laffond, 1966. pp. 22–23.
2. Ibid., pp. 23–24.
3. Ibid., pp. 47–48.
4. Ibid., p. 150.
5. Ibid., pp. 58, 163.
6. Ibid., pp. 220, 234–35.
7. Ibid., p. 240.
8. Ibid., pp. 37–38.
9. Ibid., pp. 53, 72–74.
10. Ibid., pp. 247–49, 51–52.

CHAPTER 6: HEALTH, DISEASE, SIN, AND SALVATION IN THE COMING AGE

1. Fortune, Dion. *Mystical Meditations*, pp. 187–188.

CHAPTER 7: THE PRIEST AND THE INITIATE IN THE NEW ERA

1. Fortune, Dion. *Mystical Meditations*, p. 246.

BIBLIOGRAPHY

Alighieri, Dante. *The Divine Comedy.* Translated by James Cotter. Warwick, N.Y.: Amity House, 1986.

Assagioli, Roberto. *La Vie dello Spirito.* Rome: G. Filipponio, 1974.

—*Lo Sviluppo del Transpersonale.* Rome: Astrolabio, 1988.

Bailey, Alice. *The Soul and Its Mechanism.* London: Lucis Trust, 1971.

—*From Intellect to Intuition.* London: Lucis Trust, 1971.

—*From Bethlehem to Calvary.* London: Lucis Trust, 1981.

Barnwell, F. Aster. *The Meaning of Christ for Our Age.* St. Paul: Llewellyn Publications, 1985.

—*Meditations on the Apocalypse.* Rockport, Mass.: Element Books, 1992.

Bashir, Anthon, Archbishop. *Studies in the Greek Church.* New York: Syrian, Antiochian Archdiocese, 1960.

Bedrij, Orest. *One.* San Francisco: Strawberry Hill Press, 1977.

—*You.* Warwick, N.Y.: Amity House, 1988.

Besant, Annie. *Esoteric Christianity.* New York: John Lane, 1911.

—*Ancient Wisdom.* Wheaton, Ill.: Theosophical Publishing House, 1985.

Blanquart, Henri. *Les Mystères de la Nativitié Christique.* Rennes, France: Editions Alrea, 1982.

Bucke, Richard. *Cosmic Consciousness.* New York: Dutton & Co, 1969.

Carrell, Alexis. *La Prière.* Paris: Librairie Plon, 1944.

—*L'Homme c'est Inconnu.* Paris: 1946.

Catherine of Genoa. *Purgation and Purgatory, The Spiritual Dialogue.* Classics of Western Spirituality. New York: Paulist Press, 1979.

Charpentier, Louis. *Les Mystères de la Cathèdrale de Chartres.* Paris: Robert Laffont, 1966.

Eckharthausen, Karl, von. *The Cloud Upon the Sanctuary.* New York: SRIA, 1952.

Emmanuel, R. *La Messe Vue Par les Yeux de l'Ame.* Paris: Dervy-Livres, 1976.

Ferrucci, Piero. *Inevitable Grace,* Los Angeles: Tarcher, 1990.

Fortune, Dion. *Mystical Meditations on the Collects.* London: Rider & Co., 1948.

—*The Mystical Qabalah,* London: Ernest Benn, 1957.

Griffiths, Bede, Dom. *Return to the Center.* London: Collins Fontana, 1978.

Hani, Jean. *Le Symbolisme du Temple Chrétien.* Paris: Editions de la Maisne, 1978.

Harley, Christine. *The Western Mystery Tradition.* London: Aquarian Press, 1968.

Hodson, Geoffrey. *The Hidden Wisdom in the Holy Bible.* London: Theosophical Publishing House, 1930.
—*The Inner Side of Church Worship.* Adyar, India: Theosophical Publishing House, 1930.
—*Man's Supersensory and Spiritual Powers.* Adyar, India: Theosophical Publishing House, 1957.
—*Clairvoyant Investigations into Christian Origins and Ceremonials.* Ojai, Calif.: St. Alban's Press, 1975.
—*The Priestly Ideal.* Ojai, Calif.: St. Alban's Press, 1975.
—*The Christ Life from Nativity to Ascension.* Wheaton, Ill.: Quest Books, 1975.
—*The Brotherhood of Angels and Men.* Wheaton, Ill.: Theosophical Publishing House, 1983.
John of the Cross. *Flame of Love, Spiritual Canticle.* Classics of Western Spirituality. New York: Paulist Press, 1984.
Jonas, Hans. *The Gnostic Religion.* Boston: Beacon Press, 1963.
Keating, Thomas. *Open Mind, Open Heart.* Warwick, N.Y.: Amity House, 1986.
Knight, Gareth. *A Practical Guide to Qabalistic Symbolism.* London: Helios, 1965.
Leadbeater, C.W. *The Hidden Side of Things.* Wheaton, Ill.: Theosophical Publishing House, 1974.
—*The Science of the Sacraments.* Adyar, India: Theosophical Publishing House, 1974.
—*The Christian Gnosis.* Ojai, Calif.: St. Alban's Press, 1983.
—*The Christian Creed.* Ojai, Calif.: St. Alban's Press, 1983.
—*Invisible Helpers.* Wheaton, Ill.: Theosophical Publishing House, 1985.
—*Clairvoyance.* Wheaton, Ill.: Theosophical Publishing House, 1985.
—*The Inner Side of Christian Festivals.* Ojai. Calif.: St. Alban's Press, 1986.
Legere, Thomas. *Thoughts on the Run: Glimpses of Wholistic Spirituality.* Minneapolis: Winston Press, 1983.
—*Your Spiritual Journey.* Liguori, Mo.: Liguori Publications, 1985.
Meditations on the Tarot. Rockport, Mass.: Element Books, 1991.
Meyendorff, John. *Byzantine Theology.* New York: Fordham University Press, 1978.
Needleman, Jacob. *Lost Christianity.* New York: Bantam Books, 1980.
Pagels, Elaine. *The Gnostic Gospels.* New York: Random House, 1980.
Parrish-Harra, Carol. *The Aquarian Rosary.* Tahlequah, Ok.: Village Press, 1987.
—*The Book of Rituals: Personal and Planetary Transformation.* Santa Monica: IBS Press, 1980.
Peter Dieburg of Hildesheim. *Devotio Moderna.* Classics of Western Spirituality. New York: Paulist Press, 1988.
Plummer, George (Khei). *Rosicrucian Fundamentals.* New York: Flame Press, 1920.
—*Instructions in Christian Mysticism.* New York: Mercury Publishing, 1926.
Richard of St. Victor. *The Twelve Patriarchs, The Mystical Ark, Book Three of the Trinity.* Classics of Western Spirituality. New York: Paulist Press, 1979.
Roche De Coppens, Peter. *Spiritual Man in the Modern World.* Washington: University Press of America, 1976.

—*Spiritual Perspective.* Washington: University Press of America, 1980.
—*Spiritual Perspective II: The Spiritual Dimension and Implications of Love, Sex, and Marriage.* Washington: University Press of America, 1981.
—*The Nature and Use of Ritual for Spiritual Attainment.*. St. Paul: Llewellyn Publications, 1985.
—*Apocalypse Now.* St. Paul: Llewellyn Publications, 1988.
—*The Sociological Adventure.* 2d ed. Dubuque, Iowa: Kendall-Hunt, 1990.
—*The Art of Joyful Living.* Rockport, Mass.: Element Books, 1992.
Rolle, Richard. "The Forms of Living." *The English Writings.* Translated by Rosamund S. Allen. New York: Paulist Press, 1988.
Rossner, John. *From Ancient Magic to Future Technology.* Washington: University Press of America, 1978.
—*From Ancient Religion to Future Science.* Washington: University Press of America, 1979.
—*Religion, Science, and Psyche.* Washington: University Press of America, 1979.
—*The Psychic Roots of Ancient Wisdom and Primitive Christian Gnosis.* Washington: University Press of America, 1983.
—*In Search of the Primordial Tradition and Cosmic Christ.* St.Paul St. Paul: Llewellyn Publications, 1989.
Sadhu, Mouni. *Ways to Self-Realization.* New York: The Julian Press, 1962.
—*Meditation.* London: George Allen & Unwin, 1965.
—*Theurgy.* London: George Allen & Unwin, 1969.
Sedir, Paul. *Les Guérisons du Christ.* Paris: Bibliothèques des Amitiés Spirituelles, 1953.
Smith, Huston. *Forgotten Truth: The Primordial Tradition.* New York: Harper & Row, 1976.
Sofrony, Archimandrite. *The Undistorted Image.* London: The Faith Press, 1958.
Sorokin, Pitirim. *The Ways and Power of Love.* Boston: Beacon Press, 1950.
Swedenborg, Emmanuel. *Emmanuel Swedenborg.* Classics of Western Spirituality. New York: Paulist Press, 1984.
Teresa of Avila. *The Interior Castle.* Classics of Western Spirituality. New York: Paulist Press, 1979.
Underhill, Evelyn. *Mysticism.* New York: E.P. Dutton, 1919.
—*Worship.* New York: Harper Brothers, 1937.
—*Practical Mysticism.* New York: E.P. Dutton, 1943.
Yates, Frances. *Giordano Bruno and the Hermetic Tradition.* Chicago: University of Chicago Press, 1964.